GOOD PRACTICE IN NURSERY MANAGEMENT

Elizabeth Sadek ● Jacqueline Sadek

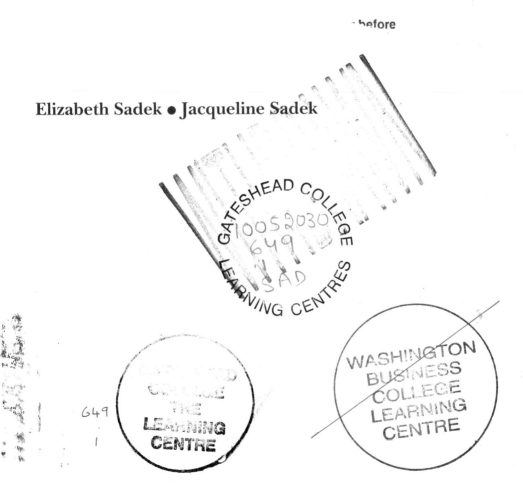

Stanley Thornes (Publishers) Ltd

First published in 1996 by:
Stanley Thornes (Publishers) Ltd
Ellenborough House
Wellington Street
CHELTENHAM GL50 1YW
United Kingdom

96 97 98 99 00 / 10 9 8 7 6 5 4 3 2

British Library Cataloguing in Publication Data

A catalogue record for this book is available from the British Library.

0–7487–2283–1

Acknowledgements

The authors and publishers would like to thank the following for permission to reproduce copyright material:

Popperfoto (p. 15); Elizabeth Handy (p. 29); Alfred A. Knopf, Inc. (p. 64); Collections/Anthea Sieveking (cover photograph).

Typeset by Columns Design Ltd, Reading
Printed and bound in Great Britain by Redwood Books, Trowbridge, Wiltshire

FOREWORD

Training in management and leadership skills for those working with under-eights has long been a neglected area – a curious oversight in view of the national obsession with raising standards in education at all levels. Yet no edifice will stand without a strong foundation, which makes the nursery experience fundamental to successful education practice.

Now, with the publication of *Good Practice in Nursery Management*, Elizabeth and Jacqueline Sadek have provided us with a foundation sound enough to support a national nursery practice and eliminate regional variations in quality of provision.

Good Practice in Nursery Management is a comprehensive manual of techniques which are currently taught in leading business schools, presented from a viewpoint and translated into a context that will be familiar to every trained early years worker. It is also a text book which provides a complete course for aspiring managers. And finally, it is a working guidebook for practising managers, showing how to comply with the latest legislation and regulations, providing check lists of key points to good practice, and sample forms and record sheets to put into immediate use.

I hope that *Good Practice in Nursery Management* will be seen, well thumbed, in nurseries, schools and colleges throughout the UK for many years to come.

David Peck
Publisher, *Nursery World*
February 1996

DEDICATION

My thanks are offered to the many groups of students on the AMC, CPQS and DPQS courses, and latterly the ADCE course, who have taught me all I know.

Elizabeth Sadek

CONTENTS

IMPORTANT NOTE TO READERS

This book aims to promote good practice in the nursery. To this end, a large number of sample policies, contracts and job descriptions have been included in Appendix A. These precedent documents may be suitable for use in certain cases but must be amended to suit appropriate circumstances. It is important to be aware that the level of skill required to amend a document may be equal to that to draft it, and that advice should in general be obtained from the local authority's Social Services Registration Officer before attempting amendments. The authors and publishers accept no responsibility for any loss occasioned to any person using or relying on any of the material in this book.

INTRODUCTION

This book is about developing the skills and strategies needed to run a nursery in the 1990s and – hopefully – into the new millennium.

A general view exists that there is an '*art of management*' lying rather uncomfortably alongside a '*science of management*'. The nature of what is being managed rather decides which of these camps individual managers fall into. Managing a nursery is very different from managing a toy factory, even if they are both child centred.

The 'science' part refers to the paper base of the manager's role: the accounts, the rotas and the book-work. The 'art' on the other hand refers to the people base of the manager's role: liaising work, personnel functions and customer relations. Charles Handy in *The Gods of Management* says 'management of organisations is not a precise science but more of a creative and political process owing much to the prevailing culture and tradition in that place at that time'. In this respect, a nursery is no different from any other organisation.

When nursery staff are promoted to be managers it is usually because they are good at looking after children and, precisely because they are good with the children, they are also good at the art part of the management task. It is supposed, because they know their job with the children, they can manage other people who don't know that job so well, or who have not been doing it for so long. Fortunately, this supposition is not altogether unfounded and, by and large, the manager will be the most competent and skilled worker on the nursery staff.

The skills already developed to manage children transfer quite well to those needed to manage staff and the strategies used to organise the childrens' lives and development do provide good background experience for the task of organising staff and staff development. There are other similarities which will emerge during discussion of management theories and the work of the manager.

Where the child care manager may have limited experience is of the science part: the administrative work, the fees, the records and the registration. However, it is likely that in this day and age most nursery workers will have at least switched on a computer – even if only for a child's developmental programme – and will be able to find help to develop administrative skills in this area. Further help may also be available from local sources and systems can readily be developed to meet the needs of small centres. Larger centres will be able to afford administrative assistance.

Transferable skills may also be available from such workaday activities as organising parents' meetings, fund raising and so forth. Expertise in pure 'business' type areas like marketing, book-keeping, managing the waiting list, doing the staff rota, external liaison and so forth can and must be developed or strategies to delegate these tasks must be devised. To help with this, an appendix is included containing samples of the paper base of the nursery manager's task.

In our profession, the move from a child care worker to nursery manager is not so dramatic as a similar shift in other professions – medicine or teaching, for example.

In being a child care worker you have:

- team experience
- people experience (even if it is with very small people)
- experience of supervising students and volunteers
- experience of being 'in charge' (even if only in charge of very small people).

So you – as a child care worker – do have a good start in management skills.

This book aims to:

- refine the skills you already hold
- explore general management theories and identify where your skills fit into these theories
- outline the areas of legal and other responsibilities of a nursery manager
- provide sample documentation for all areas of the work
- provide activities and exercises designed to further develop the concepts discussed.

The book is written as a text book for students on management courses and as a guide book for working managers who have not had the benefit of specific training courses and may be seeking alternative recognition, such as NVQ at level IV.

As a child care worker you will be familiar with and subscribe to the underlying principles and assumptions which form the value base of child care. These principles can be applied by:

- demonstrating a caring and considerate attitude towards children and parents
- recognising the crucial role that parents play and working in partnership with them wherever possible
- meeting all aspects of children's development needs
- treating and valuing children as individuals
- enabling children to be directors of their own learning
- promoting equality of opportunity
- celebrating cultural diversity
- using language that is accessible and appropriate
- sharing information and liaising with parents and other professionals
- ensuring the health and safety of children and others.

The move from managing children to managing a centre will undoubtedly cause you some discomfort. You will sooner or later find your deeply held beliefs in conflict with the pressure of your job, i.e you will experience *role conflict*. You will need to give a great deal of thought as to what exactly being a manager means and set this against the underlying principles inherent in your occupational background.

The dictionary definition of 'management' is 'the act of managing; administration; the skilful employment of means'. In this book management is viewed more as a sensible working pattern of support, intuition and reason, including systems and administration.

You, as a manager, need to give some thought to your own perspective of the role: your own style and your own ways of doing things. The parallel with child care work is again evident because each manager, like each child care worker, has their own individual way ways of working.

The role of the manager is to:

- ensure that the children are given a quality service of care
- support and supervise the staff who deliver this service
- consult and respect the wishes of the children's parents/carers
- provide adequate resources in the nursery to enable the service to function
- set up a rich and stimulating environment in which the service can be delivered
- undertake external liaison and fulfil an ambassadorial function
- be a role model for staff and children.

While this may seem a tall order, remember that there is no *single* right way to achieve all this although (also like child care) there are *multiple* wrong ways.

The aim of this book is to help you spot a wrong way before you travel too far along that path – or when that does happen, to encourage you to forgive yourself and to provide some suggestions about the return journey.

Elizabeth Sadek
Jacqueline Sadek
West London, December 1995

1 THE ROLE OF THE MANAGER IN CHILD CARE

What this chapter covers:
- responsibility of parents/carers
- local authority Children's Charter
- implications of the parent–child relationship for the manager's role
- legislation
- registration requirements

This first chapter is about the context of management in child care: the complex legal and technical relationships which impinge on the manager in a child care setting, whether day care, play group, school or special unit.

Among these complex relationships the first and most significant is the relationship with the parent and child. Another is the relationship between the manager and the various inspectors and officials who take the overall responsibility for scrutinising the provision of children's services in this country.

Responsibility of parents/carers

In providing care for children it will help the manager, first, to be clear about who the clients/customers are. Without a doubt, the clients or purchasers of our service are the parents/carers. Parents/carers after the 1989 Children Act can no longer be seen as having rights as such in respect of their child or of having *rights* over their child. They now have *responsibilities* toward their child. Where a child's parents were or have been married to each other at or after the time of the child's conception they each have parental responsibility. Otherwise the mother alone has parental responsibility unless the father acquires it by court order, i.e. by making a parental responsibilities agreement (not available before the 1989 Children Act).

It is the parent/carer's responsibility to ensure that the child is cared for. If for any reason parents are unable to carry out this responsibility it will be assumed by the Director of Social Services, or by some other person identified by a legal agent and making a claim to take this responsibility – an aunt or grandparent for instance although it need not be a blood relative under the Children Act.

PARENTAL RESPONSIBILITIES

These are defined as 'all rights, duties, powers, responsibilities and authority which by law a parent of a child has in relation to the child:
- not to harm, neglect or abandon their child, i.e. care for/show interest in the child

- to give physical and moral protection to the child
- to be legally responsible for the child's actions.

So the parent/carer has the responsibility to provide appropriate care for the child and will have different views about what might be most appropriate. Under the Act this decision and responsibility is theirs and theirs alone. If they take guidance from experts, such as school or nursery staff, it is their choice to do so.

The parents' views on child rearing are therefore most important and, being practical, it is best for business that every step is taken to recognise and respect the heavy responsibility the parents carry.

In recognition of this, the Act determines that we should work with 'parents as partners' which, from a child care point of view, seems a sensible arrangement. However, from a management point of view, a true partnership is not really an option as the parents are our *clients*. We are *working for them* and if we *work with them* it is in the best interest of *working more competently for them.*

Parents, being the purchasers of the service we provide, are our clients/employers and in management terms should be viewed in that light, i.e. we work for them to help them carry out their responsibility to their child. We must seek to supply the particular type of care and education they demand for their child – particularly the pre-school child – or they will simply take their business and child elsewhere.

The new phenomenon of the corporate nursery is evidence of the emergence of this parent power, as is the demand for educational input. Parents no longer see care alone as adequate for their child and in this they are supported by the Schools Curriculum Assessment Authority. The specially devised pre-school curriculum

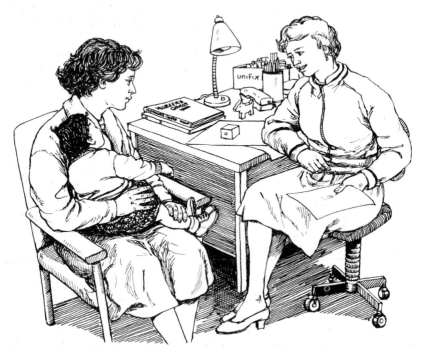

Discussion between the nursery manager and the parents is vital

which will be dealt with in Chapter 6.

It is incumbent on the centre to develop a care and educational programme which parents will find desirable and which also satisfies the developmental needs of the children. The model must then be marketed to the clients (parents) and potential clients. This situation pertains whether the nursery is in the private or public sector.

PURCHASER AND PROVIDER MODEL

Many Social Services departments have developed a purchaser-provider model of social services. This model means that they no longer run their own services – for the elderly, or special needs, or child care. They see themselves as purchasers and others as 'providers'.

The nursery is a provider and may negotiate a contract with Social Services to provide for a set number of children. In this case the authority will also take an interest and offer guidance on the services provided. They may also expect parents' extended visits to the nursery, some instruction of parents, staff attendance at case reviews and other similar additional services.

THE RIGHTS OF THE CHILD

Children represent a different challenge to management because they are not the purchasers but they are the consumers of the service. This is a fairly unique situation brought into sharp focus by the Children Act and made more interesting because under the United Nations (UN) Convention, ratified by the UK in 1991, children have *recognisable rights*.

These rights were identified by the UN Convention in a series of articles or statements. They are relevant to child care staff because during the period for which they carry the parents' responsibility, they have the duty to guard the children's rights as their parents do at all times.

INTERNATIONAL RIGHTS OF THE CHILD

Children's international rights have had some recognition since the early part of this century. In 1924 the League of Nations officially adopted the Declaration of the Rights of the Child. The League of Nations later became the UN and made a second Declaration of the Rights of the Child (1959). During the International Year of the Child (1979), Poland proposed a Convention on the Rights of the Child which was passed by the UN General Assembly in 1989.

The Convention is only binding on those countries who by signing agree to ratify it and are prepared to meet it's provisions and obligations. Until this time no test case has been brought to the UN. The UK government ratified this convention on 16 December 1991.

The Convention on the Rights of the Child exists to protect the right of the child in the community with other members of his or her group, to enjoy his or her culture, to profess and practice his or her own religion, or to use his or her own language.

Some sections of Article 3 are quoted in full below, as from a day care view point it is the most important part of the Convention.

Article 3

(a) In all actions concerning children, whether undertaken by public or private social welfare institutions, courts of law, administrative authorities or legislative bodies, the best interest of the child shall be a primary consideration.

(b) States shall undertake to ensure the child such protection and care as is necessary for his or her well being, taking into account the rights and duties of his or her parents, legal guardians, or other individuals legally responsible for him or her, and to this end, shall take all appropriate legislative measures.

(c) States shall ensure that the institutions, services and facilities responsible for the care or protecting of children shall conform with the standards established by competent authorities, particularly in areas of safety, health in the number ... of their staff as well as competent supervision.

However, various other sections are also important for us to note.

Article 5 states the duty to respect the rights and responsibilities of parents and the wider family to provide guidance appropriate to the child's evolving capacities.

Article 12 states that children must have a right to express their views on all matters affecting them with 'the views of the child being given due weight in accordance with the age and maturity of the child'.

Article 14 has two important clauses:

(a) The child's right to freedom of thought, conscience and religion, subject to appropriate parental guidance and national law.

(b) The state shall respect the rights and duties of the parents and, when applicable, legal guardians, to provide direction to the child in the exercise of his or her right in a manner consistent with the evolving capacities of the child.

Article 30 states that in places in which ethnic, religious or linguistic minorities or persons of indigenous origin exist, a child belonging to such a minority or who is indigenous shall not be denied the right, in community with other members of his or her group, to enjoy and practice his or her own religion, or to use his or her own language.

Although the UK ratified the convention an enactment was later introduced which endorses family cultural rights at the expense of children's rights. This reform was justified on the grounds that it secures parents' rights to determine their children's religious and cultural upbringing.

The reform means that children are in danger of their rights being breached at

Activity

Undertake a survey of the local authority's information services to discover whether recognition is given to the UN Convention on the Rights of the Child.

the hands of their parents or at their parents' wishes. This is a complex area and has been examined only briefly in the *context* of the manager's role.

In this country The 1989 Children Act, which is dealt with in Chapter 4, brought together nearly all aspects of the law relating to children and took cognisance of their rights. It encompasses the UN convention. Under this Act agencies are expected to give due consideration to a child's religious persuasion, racial origin, cultural and linguistic background, whilst protecting children from suffering significant harm in accordance with the UN convention and the prevailing political climate.

SUMMARY OF THE MAIN PRINCIPLES OF THE 1989 CHILDREN ACT

- The welfare of the child is the paramount consideration in court proceedings.
- Wherever possible children should be brought up and cared for within their own families.
- Children should be safe and be protected by effective intervention if they are in danger.
- When dealing with children, courts should ensure that delay is avoided and may only make a court order if it positively benefits the child.
- Children should be kept informed about what is happening to them and should participate when decisions are made about their future.
- Parents continue to have parental responsibility for their children even when their children are no longer living with them.
- Parents with children in need should be helped to bring up their children themselves. This help should be provided as a service to the child and the family and should:
    - be agreed with parents
    - meet each child's identified needs
    - be appropriate to the child's race, culture, religion and language.

Activity

This activity is designed to develop understanding of the key relationships and the context of the child care task.

(a) Discuss:
    who are the child care customers?
    who are the child care consumers?
(b) List the characteristics of a child care customer.
(c) List the characteristics of a child care consumer.

Local authority Children's Charter

Following the ratification of the UN Charter and the Children Act, many, but not all, local authorities have devised and published a Children's Charter. Here is an extract from a fairly typical publication:

- Children's welfare and their rights to a secure, healthy and happy childhood are paramount.
- The experiences children receive in their early years are critically important in terms of future development.
- Children are entitled to expect that all adults will respect, uphold and preserve their rights and ensure that their stated feelings and wishes are taken into account.
- Children should have the opportunity to make choices and develop a sense of responsibility for their own actions appropriate to their age.
- Children, parents and carers should not be discriminated against, particularly in relation to colour, race, religion, gender, disability, medical conditions or background.
- Parents should be recognised and respected as children's first and continuing educators.
- Parents and carers have the right to be consulted as partners in any decision-making process related to children in their care.

GOOD PRACTICE

A supply of copies of your local authority Children's Charter should be held for the information of staff and parents and as a reminder to everyone of the true picture.

Implications of the parent–child relationship for the manager's role

The nature of the legal relationships between parents and child impinges on the work of any school or child care centre and those who operate them. The younger and more dependent the child, the more sensitive the situation.

The children use or consume child care services – they do not choose them for themselves nor do they meet the cost. They have rights which staff are legally bound to guard but no responsibilities towards staff in terms of financial remuneration.

The parents clearly hold the legal responsibility for their children. They choose the school or nursery and they fund the service. They personally do not enjoy the care; they do not grow through the education. They can judge whether they are getting value for money only from the pattern of their child's behaviour and the fleeting impressions they receive when delivering and collecting their children.

GOOD PRACTICE

It is vital that all staff fully understand this situation. There are strong implications for staff development and staff supervision. The issues of responsibilities and rights have both philosophical and psychological aspects and deserve much further exploration in a team setting.

Parents' impressions of the nursery are clearly important

In the nursery

There is a need to develop procedures or systems which ensure that the role of the parents is always recognised and any breakdown in the system which guards the parent's role is signalled immediately to the manager so that remedial action can be taken. It is vital that the staff understand the context of their work.

See Sample 22, page 183.

Legislation

It is the responsibility of the manager to be familiar with both local and national publications outlining relevant legislation.

GOOD PRACTICE

It is useful to keep an up-dated file of the legislation for use with parents and staff and to hold the name of an expert who is available as a resource to answer questions should the need arise.

LEGISLATION RELATING TO CHILDREN

Legislation relating to children in this country has a long and painful history. Every Act passed has been a knee-jerk reaction to some dreadful incident of abuse perpetrated against a child. Such incidents provoke public outcry and precipitate action on the part of outraged individuals or hastily formed pressure groups and culminate in a law change argued through parliament by impassioned activists.

Early this century, the Barnardo Bill was the result of the death of a London orphan John Sommers, or 'Carrots' as he was known (his hair colouring being the only thing to single him out and ensure his absence caused comment).

The 1948 Act was the result of the death of Dennis O'Niell, one of a family of three children placed in foster care on a farm during wartime conditions and lost in the agency's administration until he was found dead of abuse and neglect.

The 1974 Act was the result of the death of Maria Colwell, a little seven-year-old removed from a loving foster home only to die in the midst of her own family despite the involvement of every child care agency in Brighton!

The 1989 Act was the result of the death of Jasmine Beckford and a series of other similar preventable tragedies as well as other widespread and much publicised difficulties.

On each of these tragic occasions the desire on the part of all the agencies has been to get it right, to make things better, to care for and protect the children. Recognition needs to be given to all the individuals who expended years of their lives and much energy on these attempts to keep the children safe, whatever the outcome and however minimal the success.

The will to educate and care for our children has apparently always been present in the UK. The 1989 Act, implemented in 1991, takes a much wider brief than any of its predecessors and was described by the Lord Chancellor as 'the most comprehensive and far reaching reform of child care law which has come before parliament in living memory'. The Act was welcomed by most workers and theorists because in fact it gave a legal impetus to changes already taking place in the field published by the National Children's Bureau and already accepted nationally as good practice.

OTHER RELEVANT LEGISLATION

Laws relating to the welfare of children are not the only legislation that nursery managers have to be aware of. They must also give heed to:
- Offices, Shops and Railway Premises Act (1963)
- Equal Pay Act (1970)
- Food Hygiene (General) Regulations (1970)
- Health and Safety at Work Act (1974)
- Sex Discrimination Act (1975)
- Race Relations Act (1976)
- Disabled Persons Act (1986)
- Food Safety Act (1990)
- Food Hygiene Amendment Regulation (1990).

This long list of legislation, however, does not dominate the life and work of a nursery in the same way as the 1989 Children Act. These legislative controls are applied to all employers and do not have vocational content nor offer guidance in our professional task as the Children Act undoubtedly does.

A sensible arrangement is to hold on file a copy of all the relevant parts of the above legislation to ensure a check can be made at any time.

HEALTH AND SAFETY AT WORK ACT

The Health and Safety at Work Act 1974 details the necessary requirements and places duties on employers and employees in the promotion of health, safety and welfare of persons at work. The Act also extends to those not in the employ of the organisation, i.e. children, visitors, outside contractors etc.

Sections 7 and 8 of the Act are of particular relevance to employees and are reproduced below.

Section 7

It shall be the duty of every employee whilst at work

(a) to take reasonable care for the health and safety of himself/herself and of other persons who may be affected by his/her acts or omissions at work; and

(b) as regarding duty or requirement imposed on his/her employer or any other person by or under any of the relevant statutory provisions, to co-operate with him/her as is necessary to enable that duty or requirement to be performed or complied with.

Section 8

No person shall intentionally or recklessly interfere with or misuse anything provided in the interests of health, safety or welfare in pursuance of any of the relevant statutory provisions.

Registration requirements

The Nurseries and Childminders Act 1948 requires nurseries (part-time and full-time), childminders and playgroups to be registered by local authorities. The purpose is to ensure the children's general well being; i.e. their health and safety and the quality of physical and mental development available to them. Therefore, the local authority will need to consider premises requirements, staffing ratios and the training qualifications and experience of the care givers.

The registration or the annual inspection process is comprehensive and time consuming, requiring personal inspection of sites by:

■ the social services
■ the fire department
■ the environmental health department
■ police checks on staff.

Inevitably these procedures can be subject to delays. Police checking is one area where the response time can be slow, which means a delay between the application for, and the granting of, registration.

Police checks on staff mean that no unchecked person can be left unsupervised in the nursery. Some authorities also charge for police checks which can be a financial drain on some nurseries. In this case it is advisable to ask the member of staff to pay for the check and, assuming all is well and the colleague remains in the post for an agreed period of time, the cost can then be refunded.

SOCIAL SERVICES

In many local authorities where the purchaser–provider model is not in place, the staff responsible for the registration process are also responsible for supervising the council's own child care facilities. This can cause these staff a conflict of interest and put considerable pressure on the existing resources. The pressure is likely to increase in the future as the number of applications for registration, or requests for guidance in setting up a child care facility, is expected to rise for both economic and parenting reasons as we have already discussed. The local authority will supply a standard form which asks for details such as space, staff, children's ages, opening hours and so forth. Most under-fives Local Authority Managers involved in the registration process feel it is important to be able to support people wishing to register facilities throughout the setting up process with both advice and information. This service has cost implications which will be met by the nurseries.

THE FIRE AUTHORITY

The two main Acts on fire safety are:
■ The Fire Services Act 1947
■ The Fire Precautions Act 1971 as amended by the Fire Safety and Safety of Places of Sport Act 1987.

The Fire Services Act 1947 requires fire authorities to give advice on fire safety when requested. This advice is available free of charge to any person or regulatory authority who requests it. Fire officers will inspect premises at the request of social services departments to advise on their suitability for the purposes of day care. Social services departments should encourage day care providers to approach their local fire brigade for advice on fire safety.

The Fire Precautions Act 1971 covers fire precautions in occupied premises and is administered by fire authorities. Under this Act all nurseries require a fire certificate which will specify fire precautions such as:
■ the means of escape
■ fire fighting equipment
■ means of warning in the event of fire.

The fire brigade has to ensure that any statutory requirements made under the Fire Precautions Act are complied with.

Fire drill procedures should be displayed and made accessible to all nursery users, parents, volunteers, students and staff. Regular fire drills should take place, particularly after the appointment of new staff or the arrival of new students.

It is a general requirement attached to fire certificates that all people who work in buildings for which a fire certificate is required shall be given instruction and training to ensure that they understand the fire precautions and action to be taken in the event of fire. The training should include people on regular duties or shift duties working outside normal working hours, including all part time staff, cleaners and so forth. These arrangements must take account of the special needs of anyone likely to be in the premises, e.g. anyone with a physical handicap.

Of course, sensible fire precautions and good housekeeping practices will reduce the possibility of having a fire and needing to evacuate the building.

KEYS TO GOOD PRACTICE

- Parents must be welcomed in the nursery at all times.
- Parents must be kept informed of all aspects of the children's activities.
- Parents' role in their children's lives must be respected in all professional liaison.
- Children should be respected as individuals in the context of their race, culture and language.
- Children should be allowed to be directors of their own learning.
- All staff should be aware of the wider legal requirements of the centre and understand the context of their job.
- All staff should be familiar with local authority regulations and the Children's Charter.
- All staff should be competent in fire drill procedures.

2 MANAGEMENT THEORIES APPLIED TO THE CHILD CARE SERVICE

> **What this chapter covers:**
> - the importance of research
> - research methodologies
> - organisational behaviour
> - structure, function and cultures in the work place

The aim of this chapter is to define *organisational behaviour* and to set the scene in child care terms to that part of management theory generally referred to as 'structures, functions and cultures'.

Most of the theoretical research in this area has been undertaken in industrial and commercial settings – as part of the work of industrial psychologists or of organisational behaviour specialists (who are working from a psychological base). There has been very little direct management research undertaken in child care settings. However, many industrial theoretical studies provide useful analytical tools for any manager. Briefly, we aim to examine how research is undertaken in this area and how much value we give research, before we look at how organisations/centres are arranged (structured) and how such arrangements can help or hinder the functioning of the centre, the jobs and the satisfaction of the staff. Clearly this will all have an impact on the quality of the service provided to customers (in this case, the parents/carers) and to consumers (in this case, the children).

The importance of research

WHAT IS MEANT BY 'THEORY'?

Throughout this text theories will be offered for consideration. It would be helpful to be clear about what exactly a theory is – because even well-founded and accepted theories do not contain absolute truths and are not written in tablets of stone. A theory is simply an idea that one person (a theorist) has put forward to explain some observed behaviour or patterns of behaviour in individuals in groups and in organisations.

CASE STUDY

The photocopier in an office will not give up its paper.
Someone has a theory (a) that the paper feeder is jammed. Evidence to support this theory is that in this individual's observation of other such occasions, the paper feeder was found to be jammed. Someone else has a

theory (b) that the machine is switched off. Evidence to support this theory is also observation, i.e. that the plug is lying under the machine and is not plugged in to the socket.

The weight of evidence for the second theory is irrefutable. Of course, the paper feeder may also be jammed, but that is not the most scientific explanation of the failure available at this point in time.

A theory is an idea offered to explain a phenomenon. It is not the theory as such but the evidence to support the theory that is the crucial element in the equation. Some theorists base their ideas on observation alone – Charles Darwin observed the world for years and came up with the 'Theory of Evolution'; Jean Piaget observed his own children over a much shorter period and came up with the 'Theory of Consistency'. A Greek philosopher named Archimedes got into a bath, observed the change in the water level and in a single instant leapt out shouting 'Eureka' and came up with the 'Theory of Displacement', also known as Archimedes' Principle. He no doubt then spent many weeks explaining the theory in complicated mathematics. It was the mathematics as well as the bath that he offered as evidence. In using other people's theories it is vital to look at the evidence they produce to support the theory.

The idea or theory has to be expressed as a hypothesis or prediction. For example:

'the photocopier will jam if you use the wrong type of paper'

or

'children will grow in confidence if given praise as a reward'.

Darwin's hypothesis was that organisms evolve towards specialisms by the principle of the survival of the fittest. To support his hypothesis he collected evidence. He travelled the seas and by examining various animal species he conceived the notion of 'natural selection' which ensured the 'survival of the fittest'. By this he meant that the best equipped individuals of any species, with all their strengths, survived long enough to reproduce and pass their genes to the next generation. He recorded his observations over many years until he was convinced that his evidence supported his theory and proved his hypothesis.

ORGANISATIONAL THEORY

The theories we will be using are in essence no different from this. They are sometimes called management theories and sometimes organisation theories. This latter term is the most useful.

In order to manage it is valuable to be able to predict what might happen next based on what is happening now or what happened yesterday, even if it happened to someone else. If you know what is likely to happen next you can organise yourself, your colleagues and staff to deal with that event.

Charles Handy (1992) tells us that organisation theory:

'helps one to explain the past which, in turn
helps one to understand the future which
leads to more influence over future events and to
suffer less disturbances from the unexpected'.

It will help a manager to have some grasp of organisation theory. A theory is only of use if it is supported by evidence or if it is known to what extent the evidence supplied is weak or indeed non-existent. Theories with non-existent evidence are either:

(a) new theories not yet proven or
(b) models or (paradigms) of reality – one person's or group's ideas of how the world is arranged.

An example of this second type of theory is R. Meredith Belbin's 'Theory of Team Roles' (1981), which is discussed in Chapter 7.

Paradigms or *models* are also often used in managerial studies and can be of great service when analysing a new situation.

A good example of this is McKinsey's seven S's, which is one way of diagrammatically representing the role and tasks of the manager. This model is particularly pertinent in child care because shared values underpin our work just as they do in McKinsey's model. The model aims to illustrate the variables which managers must deal with when planning their work. It is organised in seven S's for easy recall. You will see that the listed areas of concern here are similar to the areas we will discuss.

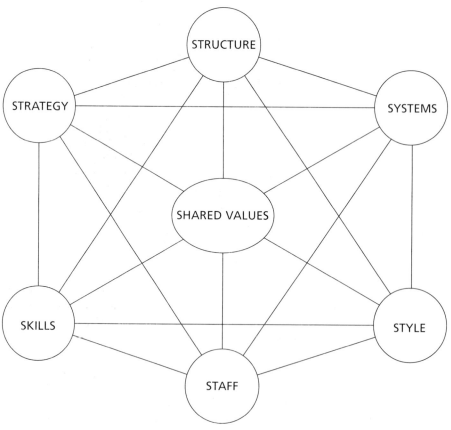

McKinsey's model of the role and tasks of the manager

- Shared values
- Staff support and motivation
- Skills needed for the child care task
- Strategies – the plans we make for areas of the work
- Structure – of the nursery – what makes it work
- Systems – for care of records
- Style – leadership style which is most appropriate for child care

Models and weaker evidence theories may be used and quoted and may be very helpful to managers.

However, these theories are unlike the 'Theory of Gravity', for example, which embodies an absolute truth and will predict results accurately every time. Every object thrown up will come down again at some time attracted by the earth's gravitational pull. The evidence for the 'Theory of Gravity' is irrefutable – it can be proved mathematically, by scientific experiment and can be explained by the rational laws of nature.

Charles Darwin (1809–1882)

The evidence for Darwin's 'Theory of Evolution' is not so strong. It is based entirely on observation of natural phenomena and explained by an imaginative construct. It could only be proven by scientific experiment if it were possible to reproduce in the laboratory the whole of the history of the planet and the development of organic life.

When Darwin first published his theory he was held up to ridicule by almost all his colleagues in the field, most of the general public and every religious activist. However, as time passed the number of individuals arguing against his theory became fewer and fewer. People have become intellectually accustomed to Darwin's construct and where it once seemed alien, it now makes perfect sense.

Research methodologies

Research methodologies can take various forms as outlined below.

OBSERVATIONS

This method records what happens in the real world and discovers how actions are perceived by those involved. The two main types of observation are:
- open or overt method: those observed are aware of the observation
- participant observer method: in this case the researcher becomes a member of the group and takes part in its activities, often without the other participants knowing the primary reason for this individual's presence.

SOCIAL SURVEYS

A survey is usually a verbal questionnaire or form of interview used to gain information from large numbers of people. It is often undertaken in the street, and is particularly associated with consumables.

QUESTIONNAIRES

These are written lists of questions pertaining to the research and are sent to a large number of selected people.

INTERVIEWS

These may be:
- formal structured interviews: either questionnaires read out by an interviewer with boxes to tick with the appropriate choice from 5 or 6 answers, or a series of pre-arranged questions which can be answered in open unpredicted way
- informal interviews: characterised by open questions. Interviewers may even follow up answers with further relevant enquiries.

DIARIES

Respondents are asked to keep a daily journal of events and feelings, over a particular length of time.

LIFE HISTORY

This could be a complete biography of someone or it could be aimed at major events in the person's life.

TIME-BUDGETING

This is used to discover how people structure their day and what they do at certain times, e.g. to determine how shift work affects peoples lives. This is best done over a relatively short period of time as it can be time consuming for the respondents.

CASE STUDY

This is usually an in-depth study of a person or situation using interview techniques and some observations.

COMMUNITY STUDY

This could be a study of a particular area or group. It could involve participant obser-vation, interviewing and literature search methods.

EXPERIMENTS

Experiments are used to try and find out if one event causes another. The researcher has to try to examine one variable while keeping other factors the same. Experiments are of two types:

- laboratory experiments. These involve investigations where experimenters try and look at one particular aspect of behaviour under controlled conditions
- field experiments. These are experiments that take place in the real world. Those taking part may not be aware of the fact. Rosenthal and Jacobson's (1968) exper-iment to see the effect of teachers' expectations on pupils' performances found that if teachers thought pupils would do well, they treated them differently and their subsequent performance improved.

Organisational behaviour

Organisational theory is used to explain how organisations work. The term organi-sational theory has been widely used in the last 100 years, but the activity itself dates back to the Ancients – the Greeks and Chinese (we have inherited many useful insights from these sources). Sometimes the term industrial psychology is used to describe this activity, although this term also has more restrictive uses.

Generally the organisational behaviour theories come from three perspectives:

- the organisational structure and functions
- the systems and procedures designed to cope with transactions and interactions in the organisation, and
- the individuals who work there.

The whole study of management is fraught with complexity. Theorists in this area are simply unable to competently control the many variables which confront them – no two people, no two situations are alike, nor can they be easily reproduced to test and re-test the findings.

Much of the evidence offered by management theorists will be based on

- observations, like those of Charles Darwin or the Hawthorne experiment
- experiments, like those of Rosenthal and Jacobson (1968)
- retrospective case studies, like those of Holmes and Rahe (1967)
- one person's notion or good idea, like 'open book management'
- models or paradigms which when shared with others have a certain common sense appeal, like Maslow (1954).

These last two types of theory are easy to argue against or to prove invalid simply because they have not been adequately tested. However, if used with an open mind, such constructs are very useful as long as their status is well understood.

Structure, function and cultures in the workplace

STRUCTURE

The term 'structure' refers to the way an organisation is formally put together -the official picture – who is the boss and who reports to whom.

The structure of an organisation depends on two important things:

- **purpose**, i.e. goals and objectives – what the company does/makes/sells/services
- **size**

and also on a series of much less significant things such as the history, the ownership, the staff, the economic climate, environmental factors and so forth.

Structure is usually presented diagrammatically for marketing purposes in literature published by many quite small organisations and by all large ones. This perception of the organisation may not be exactly as a management theorist would describe it.

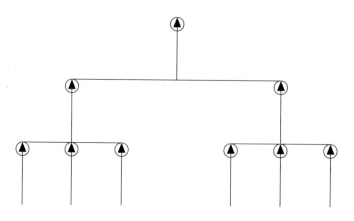

A typical hierarchy model used by a manager

Purpose, goals and objectives

'Purpose' in child care terms can be illustrated by the difference between managing a centre where the children are well, happy and busy with their development and managing a centre caring for sick children or children at risk.

Management techniques in these two different centres will be differently focused, emergency procedures differently arranged, reporting systems tighter; the aim in one being to educate and care for the children, and in the other being to protect them and facilitate medical or social intervention. *A happy, relaxed and informal structure will prevail in one and a calm carefully controlled, formalised and monitoring structure in the other.*

When studying general management theory you will find the contrasts drawn between managing a hospital and managing a lawyers office – that is, between a large complex bureaucratic structure and a 'look out for yourself' structure.

Size

Size is the single most important factor affecting both the structure of an organisation and its cultures. Most child care centres are very small in management terms.

Nonetheless managing a 60 place children's centre operated by the local authority will be very different from managing a 20 place unit for a corporate nursery or a 30 place owner-run nursery or again managing a work-based nursery.

TYPES OF STRUCTURE AND CULTURE

Structure theorists, including Max Weber (1921) who first described bureaucracy, and Roger Harrison (1972), together with the British theorist, Charles Handy (1986), detail four main structures and cultures. They are generally called bureaucracy, autocracy, matrix and cluster structures and role, power, task and person cultures.

The structure of each organisation is often associated with a certain culture or way of behaving.

Child care centres can be found without too much effort which well illustrate each one of these structures and cultures.

Bureaucratic structure and role culture:
- local authorities including nurseries (social and educational)
- some of the large corporate nurseries
- sometimes work-based nurseries

(Note: in modern usage, the word 'bureaucracy' is seen as a negative term; here it is used as a neutral term. Many workers enjoy the bureaucratic structure which has a great many advantages).

Autocratic structure and power culture:
- owner-managed nurseries
- small private schools
- some playgroups

Matrix structure and task culture:
- some work-based nurseries
- some playgroups
- community nurseries

(Community run nurseries often work like this. Although someone is the boss, everyone has an apparently equal say and there is no real power base or the power base is shared.)

Cluster structure and person culture:

■ some emergency nanny agencies
■ groups of self-employed childminders
■ some individual units within corporate nursery groups

(In this structure, everyone is doing their own thing, running their own show but collecting work and support centrally from each other and using services which are collectively funded.)

ORGANISATIONAL CULTURE

The notion of organisational culture or way of behaving was first described by Roger Harrison; he used the word 'ideology' but 'culture' is now in more common use. We retain the names he gave to describe each type of culture. He identified four:

■ role ideology or culture
■ power ideology or culture
■ task ideology or culture
■ person ideology or culture.

In any organisation, and that includes nurseries, groups of individuals over time develop ways of doing things – deep set beliefs about what is and what is not an acceptable way of working. These beliefs or norms of behaviour are what in this context is described as 'culture' and are a reflection of the same concept used to describe societies.

The culture of the organisation will affect what people are called (first or second names), how they are dressed (formal or informal dress code), how they work with the children and how they relate to the parents, the registration officer and any other person associated with the nursery.

Like structure, the culture of an organisation is dependent on both purpose and on size.

CASE STUDY

New staff joining such organisational cultures are given, either formally or informally (depending on the structure), an induction into 'the Anywhere way'.

'As a new member of staff in a very famous nursery I foolishly made a surprised comment on the expert performance of two-year-olds with their knives and forks. I was rebuked by the remark "we like good table manners, it is the Anywhere way". A colleague took me aside and said "you'll hear a lot about the Anywhere way – it isn't written down you know, it has seeped into the brick work – you just wait until you pick it up by osmosis". Later, one parent told me that her child was totally incapable of using a knife and fork at home – certainly the parent did not expect her to be able to. The little girl did not take 'the Anywhere way' home with her.'

In the situation described here, it would be very hard for a new manager to change anything. In any case, good table manners constitute desirable behaviour and this serves to illustrate that not all cultural traditions demand change. The other interesting lesson to be learned from this example is the wonder of a small child, who at two years old knows that behaviour acceptable in one culture can be quite different from the behaviour acceptable in another.

This phenomenon can also be observed by students who move within schools from one room to another and find that even within the same school structure, cultures differ from room to room from staff team to staff team.

CASE STUDY

'I recall as a very junior student nurse being scolded on my first appearance on a hospital ward by a dragon of a Sister who completed her precautionary rebuke by saying "and don't think we will tolerate any of your sloppy Ward 3 ways here". Ward 3, although part of the same bureaucracy was an orthopaedic ward full of young and vigorous motorcyclists who had various broken bones but were otherwise in rude good health.

Needless to say the culture in that unit was quite different from the rest of the hospital and particularly from the acute female surgical unit presided over by the dragon.'

As this example illustrates culture, like structure, is also very much affected by the purpose of the organisation The culture in a reception class evolved to support and settle very young children differs from the culture in a secondary class designed to encourage a systematic learning environment.

It is dangerous to think that one culture is better than another. There is no right or correct culture for any organisation or any nursery any more than for a country. An individual might enjoy and feel more comfortable in one rather than in another but no culture can be right or wrong in itself. Just as individuals might be more comfortable in England than in France and more comfortable in France than in Japan, so staff will have a culture that suits them best and where they function well. The reverse is also true. People often complain of this, saying 'my face didn't fit'. They found themselves in an alien culture and unless they were prepared to change their own ways they would not fit in.

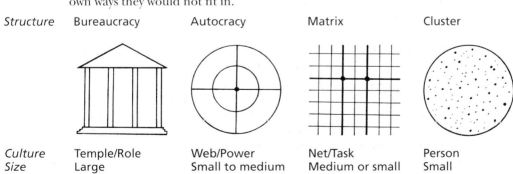

Structure	Bureaucracy	Autocracy	Matrix	Cluster
Culture	Temple/Role	Web/Power	Net/Task	Person
Size	Large	Small to medium	Medium or small	Small

Types of structure and culture

In setting out the table on page 21 the whole area has been made to look very simplistic. However, it can become very complicated, particularly when the *culture* of one part of the organisation is in conflict with the *structure* of another part of the organisation. This can easily happen, as the following Case Study illustrates.

CASE STUDY

One work-based nursery had great communication difficulties because the hospital it served had a bureaucratic structure and the nursery left to itself was autocratic. In instances like this communication becomes a major issue – one side failing to grasp the view or the needs of the other. They are genuinely coming from different cultures – neither right, neither wrong, only different.

Conversely, another large bureaucracy, a university, containing many matrices at it's edges in clusters of task-oriented academics could happily support, accommodate and communicate with a nursery which functioned as a matrix on most days and an autocracy in times of crisis.

Activity
This activity is designed to develop understanding of structures.
(a) List the factors in your centre which you think influence the structure.
(b) Working with a colleague, verbally expand on your list and then on your colleague's list.
(c) Is this it's first structure?
(d) Which structure might come next?

BUREAUCRATIC STRUCTURE, ROLE CULTURE

Bureaucracy was first described by the philosopher/sociologist and great German economist Max Weber (1921). He described it as 'the authority of the eternal yesterday'. A bureaucratic structure and it's dependent role culture is characterised by the jobs or 'roles' staff occupy, not by them as personalities, or as individuals, or even by their academic qualifications. It will be led by a Chief Executive. Two or more Deputies will be answerable to the Chief Executive and this group makes up the pinnacle of the temple in the structure diagram. The pillars or poles supporting the pinnacle represent different departments/rooms or units/centres. Each unit will have it's own leader/head of department who, in turn, will have one or two deputies who will have staff answerable to them and so forth.

Advantages of a bureaucratic structure
Role culture and bureaucratic structure prevails in stable times. It is excellent for staff development and progression. It allows ambitious talented assertive individuals to climb steadily up the pillar, to have some sense of where they are going, and how well they are doing on the journey. They can be heard making such remarks as 'I was

already a head of department by the time I was 30'. It is safe and in most instances people have jobs for life and pensions. It often provides sports facilities and other perks and is paternalistic.

Disadvantages of a bureaucratic structure

Charles Handy (1986) notes that, like the Greek temple it resembles, the pillars of a bureaucratic structure will rock and crumble causing the whole edifice to tumble when the earth shakes. Bureaucracy needs stability to survive and hates change. It is argued that bureaucracy saps individual's creativity and limits their horizons causing alienation.

AUTOCRATIC STRUCTURE, POWER (OR CLUB) CULTURE

This is the traditional shape of a company started up and run by one individual. The leader holds the reins, has all the power and gives the name to the culture. Although it is generally shown as a web – the spider in the middle making all the silk and holding all the reins of the company – it may adopt. whatever shape the power holder (the spider) feels happiest with. However much these structures vary, they have one common feature: they are dominated by one single personality (or sometimes one single family). They function by the power of personal loyalty. The quality in this culture is very much in the hands of the power holder – good or bad. Staff can only join the club or leave.

This culture is the one most reported in newspapers when it gets to be any size and runs into difficulties, particularly because there is no control of the massive driving ego. These organisations are run by moguls who are confident of getting their own way and unless they are unfortunate they generally are successful in doing so.

It is important to notice that many large bureaucracies had their origins in the autocratic club culture of one energetic individual with a good idea. Industrial historians take great delight in these famous names – Ford, Sainsbury, Cadbury, Coates, Fry.

Advantages of an autocratic structure and power/club culture

It enables very speedy decisions to be made, minimises administration and is cheap to run. Money is spent where it matters. It values individuals and gives them their freedom. The reward for success is high.

Disadvantages of an autocratic structure and power/club culture

It is nepotistic, although this is not always a bad thing. It can feel very like a 'closed shop'. It is paternalistic and cultivates the 'cult of the individual'.

MATRIX STRUCTURE, TASK CULTURE

The matrix structure and its task culture is a relatively recent phenomenon. The strength of the matrix is at the intersections – where the networks cross. The structure draws resources from various parts of the organisation to focus on the knotty problems the organisation as a whole is constantly solving. The task culture is only interested in expertise which is applied by teams with specific responsibility within overall management strategy.

This structure is common among teams of interdependent professionals, e.g. academics; architects and surveyors; film makers, make-up artists and camera staff. In this context it serves to strengthen and facilitate the work of the teams.

Corporate nurseries sometimes demonstrate this structure. Frequently a 'set up team' exists working within an organisation waiting to move to a new site, using the specialist setting up expertise and skills of purchasing, liaising with local authorities, supervising plumbers, builders and electricians etc.

Advantages of the matrix structure and task culture
It is good for people who know their job well, who are enthusiastic and committed to teams. There is no place for private agendas. It fosters mutual respect and flourishes in times of change if, and only if, the economic climate is sound.

Disadvantages of the matrix structure and task culture
It is very expensive to run. It has difficulty in developing systems and routines. It tends to be short-lived and is slow to make decisions.

CLUSTER STRUCTURE, PERSON CULTURE

This structure is usually associated with professional legal or medical practices where workers may occupy the same space but do not strictly speaking form 'teams' as each individual operates for and by himself or herself. The structure exists only to host its members.

This is the only structure in which the individual is greater than the organisation. Emergency nanny services and groups of childminders are examples of this structure.

Advantages of the cluster structure and person culture
It works well when success depends on the skill, talent and energy of members. It allows for personal identity to flourish. It allows for great flexibility and freedom and is considered to be a low-stress structure.

Disadvantages of cluster structure and person culture
There is very poor status given to some members of staff, e.g. the practice manager, administrative staff. No manager holds reward power so that members are difficult to control and there is only management by consent. If members are not satisfied they will not hang on for the sake of the organisation – they are more important than the organisation and they will simply move on. If enough of them move on, the organisation will fold up.

Activity
Work in pairs or groups of three.
(a) Make a diagram of your organisation or centre.
(b) Label it appropriately.

KEYS TO GOOD PRACTICE

- Check that the structure of the nursery is in accord with the culture.
- Check that the culture of the nursery is appropriate to its function.
- Ensure that new members of the nursery are not excluded or made to feel they do not belong.
- Appoint a mentor to support new colleagues.
- Arrange a 'friend' for new parents and children.

3 STRATEGIES FOR MANAGING QUALITY CARE

> **What this chapter covers:**
> - motivation theories
> - traditional theories of motivation
> - research studies
> - non-traditional theories of motivation
> - leadership theories

This chapter is about the main academic organisational theories which underpin management techniques:

- manager as leader
- manager as motivator
- manager as support
- manager as empowerer and, inevitably,
- manager as controller.

As has been noted, the pure research in management comes mostly from industry and spans the last century or so since the first management research was undertaken. Some of this work, particularly knowledge of the theories of motivation, is particularly pertinent because of the need to motivate children and parents, students and volunteers, in addition to the staff teams charged with delivering quality care.

Knowledge of leadership theory is pivotal to the manager's task in the nursery for it is on the manager's performance that the nursery's future and profitability depends.

Motivation theories

By motivation we mean what makes us *do* something – in this case what makes us want to work – and more specifically what makes us want to work harder.

The historical/theoretical perspective on motivation makes certain assumptions about a human being:

- He/she is a rational economic being, i.e human beings are motivated by their own needs and are self serving.
- He/she is a social being, i.e. human beings will be happier functioning within a group or team – we are gregarious/pack animals.
- He/she is a self-actualising being, i.e. human beings are self motivating or self starting and will make voluntary psychological contracts with the organisation.
- He/she is a complex being and can respond to a variety of management strategies in unpredictable ways.

■ He/she is a psychological being – this evolves from the notion of the *ideal ego state*. We all hold in our heads a model of ourselves, an 'ideal ego', which will drive us forwards to strive towards our image of the perfect self, well after needs such as hunger have been satisfied.

If work is part of the identity of the perfect self – the 'ideal ego' - then work will be undertaken constantly (this phenomenon is part of a theory sometimes referred to by sociologists as the *Protestant Work Ethic*).

'E' FACTORS

Organisational theorists have undertaken a great deal of research in this area, and have developed a motivation formula based on the notion of 'E' factors.

The 'E' in motivation theories represents:

Effort
Enthusiasm
Energy
Excitement
Expenditure
Effectiveness
Efficiency

The job of the manager as motivator is to activate or liberate as many 'E' factors in their staff teams as possible. There are a great many ways of doing this apart from the 'carrot and the stick' approach, although these methods still have their uses.

PSYCHOLOGICAL CONTRACTS

Workers have a *psychological contract* with their employers or with their organisation or with their job. (Note: we all have many such psychological contracts, e.g. with family, with children, with the darts club, with the operatic society, with the church – symbolised by the people we simply cannot let down).

Psychological contracts work well for staff motivation if:

- the psychological contract with the job is more satisfying than any other the staff member may be holding currently (it rarely competes well with a new house, a wedding or a new baby so allowances have to be made at times of major life events)
- the psychological contract is viewed identically by both staff and organisation; it can then be depended upon by both sides and becomes both predictable and useful.

There are several varieties of psychological contracts.

Coercive contracts

In a coercive contract the 'E' factors are called forth by punishment, or the fear of punishment ('the stick').

Calculative contracts

In a calculative contract the 'E' factors are called forth by reward, usually more money such as a bonus ('the carrot').

Co-operative contracts

In a co-operative contract the 'E' factors are called forth by the needs of the leader, the task or the organisation. The contract holder must therefore identify closely with the needs of the organisation, so we have the phenomena of the company man' and the 'vocational calling'.

It is not possible to force a co-operative contract on paid staff, they must pick it up by themselves. It is like responsibility – it cannot be given, it has to be taken.

The following activity will help you to work out some of your psychological contracts.

- Rank order these expectations starting with 1 as top priority, in terms of their importance to:
  - (a) the group
  - (b) yourself.
- What do you expect from them? List as many expectations as you can
- Rank order these expectations in terms of their importance to:
  - (a) yourself
  - (b) the group.

Does this tell you anything about the psychological contracts you have with these groups?

How could these contracts be different?

Who would change them?

(Adapted from Handy, 1986.)

Charles Handy   (Photo: Elizabeth Handy)

Traditional theories of motivation

There are three main traditional theories of motivation and these are discussed below.

- Satisfaction theory of motivation – where the workers' mere passive satisfaction equals their productivity.
- Incentive theory of motivation – where rewards are given which call forth 'E' factors and result in more productivity ('carrot').
- Intrinsic theory of motivation – where the job is worthwhile in its own right (in the opinion of the subject) and this will call forth 'E' factors and more productivity.

SATISFACTION THEORY OF MOTIVATION

This theory states that merely satisfied workers do not produce more, but they stay longer, and have better mental health records than those who are dissatisfied. This in turn leads to less absenteeism and a smaller staff turnover, which in child care is an extremely important characteristic.

This theory relates to the person who turns in day after day to do a fairly mundane job and works up to the time they are being paid (the 'timeserver'). However, even these workers perform better when they like their leader and are satisfied with their group or team of colleagues. Human beings are, after all, pack animals.

Where staff are generally satisfied, greater effort can be called forth and greater productivity will result if they want to help others in the team.

CASE STUDY

There are negative aspects of satisfaction theory.
Sometimes it happens that lower production than is possible will satisfy the team and output could be held down by group pressure.
'I recall a nursery unit where the supervisor was either working in her office or constantly nagging and seemingly extremely unsupportive to her staff. Nevertheless they were rarely off-sick and seemed to stay forever. The practice in the nursery was fair, good enough to keep it ticking over, but not brilliant. The place was clean but not exciting. The staff seemed sombre, they arrived and they went on the dot'.

It took a change of supervisor and some management input, but no money, to stimulate this team to transform this adequate provision into the vibrant place it is today.

INCENTIVE THEORY OF MOTIVATION

This theory states that productivity (effort) is called forth by reward (money). This will work if:

- the worker thinks the effort is worth the money
- the effort can clearly be attributed to the individual worker
- the worker wants the reward, i.e. needs the money
- any new effort will not become a new minimum production level with no extra reward attached.

This theory of motivation is rare in work with children although private nannies involved in unsocial working hours and in dangerous or difficult locations are often rewarded in this way.

INTRINSIC THEORY OF MOTIVATION

The intrinsic theory of motivation claims that a worker's own needs are motivators *when these needs are unsatisfied*. So if a worker needs to gain personal recognition by the supervisor, they will work diligently until such recognition is given. If the worker needs to be in control to hold power, they will work diligently until they get to be in charge or to hold power even if that takes a whole working life.

The intrinsic theory cannot be used if:

■ technology or structure prevents it, e.g. the worker is trapped in a structure or technology with no power to change things

■ the workers involved have no self-actualising needs, or if the worker prefers an autocratic leadership style. Note that a person's preferences may vary at different times; a young inexperienced worker may feel more secure when strong guidance is available or a worker who currently carries a lot of family responsibility may not feel able to shoulder even more at work.

This theory works best where people are self-starters, e.g. in research and development and with entrepreneurial business people.

This theory is much in evidence in small, privately owned nurseries where individual workers are self motivating. It can also be found in specialist unconventional centres, e.g. special needs units or sick children's provision.

Research studies

There are several important studies associated with motivation which have a particular significance for the child care service.

■ The Hawthorne studies (1926)
■ Maslow's hierarchy of needs (1954)
■ Herzberg's two-factor theory of motivation (1966, 1968)
■ The psychological theory of the locus of control (Rother, 1966)

THE HAWTHORNE STUDIES

In the late 1920s a group of young women who assembled telephone equipment were the subjects of a series of studies, known as the Hawthorne studies, undertaken to determine the effect on their output of working conditions, length of the working day, number and length of rest pauses, and other factors of the 'non-human' environment. The women, especially chosen for the study, were placed in a special room under one supervisor and were carefully observed.

As the experimenters began to vary the conditions of work, they found that, with each major change, there was a substantial increase in production. Being good experimenters, they decided, when all the conditions to be varied had been tested, to return the girls to their original poorly-lit work benches for a long working day without rest pauses and other amenities. To the astonishment of the researchers, output rose again, to a level higher than it had been even under the best of the experimental conditions.

At this point, the researchers were forced to look for factors other than those which had been deliberately manipulated in the experiment. For one thing, it was quite evident that the young women had developed very high morale during the experiment and had become extremely motivated to work hard and well. The reasons for this high morale were found to be:

- the young women felt special because they had been singled out for a research role; this selection showed that management thought them to be important
- the young women developed good relationships with one another and with their supervisor because they had considerable freedom to develop their own pace of work and to divide the work among themselves in a manner most comfortable for them
- the social contact and easy relations among the young women made the work generally more pleasant.

A new kind of hypothesis was formulated out of this preliminary research. The hypothesis was that motivation to work, productivity and quality of work are all related to the nature of the social relations among the workers and between the workers and their boss.

The Hawthorne studies are seminal in that not only did the experiment tell us a great deal about why people work harder but it also gave rise to an analytic tool – the so-called 'Hawthorne effect' which asks that allowance be made in observational studies if the subjects are aware they are being studied.

It is because of this work that much observational research work takes place through a two-way mirror or by participating disguised researchers.

GOOD PRACTICE

The message from the Hawthorne studies is clear: staff need to be affirmed as people who are valuable to the organisation. They need to know that an interest is taken in their work and they need praise for a job well done.

Cautionary note: it is not advisable to reward poor work, but any interest is better than no interest.

The discovery that staff work harder if someone takes an interest in their work is extremely useful for any manager in a child care setting.

CASE STUDY

'Based on the knowledge of Hawthorne, I have often set up regular meetings with staff in order for them to share their progress and to allow discussion of their work. This helps in various non-routine situations:
- if I am having difficulties adjusting to their style of working
- if we are together setting up a new venture, in this case the meetings are very frequent – probably daily
- if they are having a difficult time with some aspect of their work -the more difficult, the more frequent the meetings.

The down-side of this strategy is that it is difficult for staff to abandon the routine when the work is complete or the crisis over.'

MASLOW'S HIERARCHY OF NEEDS

Maslow developed a motivation theory based on a hierarchy of needs. These can be represented as a pyramid (see p. 33) with seven levels. Examine this pyramid closely.

```
                              SELF-
                          ACTUALISATION
                        Realising your full
                       potential, 'becoming
                          everything one is
                        capable of becoming'
                      _____
                         AESTHETIC NEEDS
                        Beauty – in art and
                        nature – symmetry,
                        balance, order, form
                    _____
                        COGNITIVE NEEDS
                    Knowledge and understanding,
                    curiosity, exploration, need
                     for meaning and predictability
                _____
                         ESTEEM NEEDS
                The esteem and respect of others AND
                   self-esteem and self-respect.
                     A sense of competence
            _____
                   LOVE AND BELONGINGNESS
               Receiving and giving love, affection,
                      trust and acceptance.
           Affiliating, being part of a group (family, friends, work)
       _____
                        SAFETY NEEDS
          Protection from potentially dangerous objects or situations,
                  e.g. the elements, physical illness.
       The threat is both physical and psychological. (e.g. 'fear of the unknown').
                   Importance of routine and familiarity
   _____
                     PHYSIOLOGICAL NEEDS
           Food, drink, oxygen, temperature regulation, elimination,
                        rest, activity, sex
```

Maslow's hierarchy of needs (based on Maslow 1954)

The most basic of these needs are the physiological – hunger, thirst, sex and so forth. The next level indicates needs that are more sophisticated than this – safety, belonging and so on. The third level is more refined still and so on until one reaches the pinnacle of needs, which he terms 'self actualisation'.

Maslow's work is regarded as basic to motivational analysis and is often quoted because it explains a great deal about human beings in all aspects of their lives.

There are, of course, opponents to the Maslow model. We can all think of exceptions: the starving artist who finds the inspiration to paint and self actualise despite hunger and the footballer who plays on and scores a goal only to discover later an injury – even a broken bone. But the fact that such exceptions are news says a lot about the general rule.

Higher level needs are a later evolutionary development in the history of the species. You will have noticed that the higher up the pyramid one goes the more needs are linked to life experience and less to biology and the more difficult they are to achieve.

Self actualisation seems to be a fairly modern concept; the more sophisticated we become the more we expect personal fulfillment.

It is important to consider Maslow's model in association with the notion discussed earlier of the psychological being, and to recognise that what actualises one person may not actualise another and that we are all complex beings.

One woman, for example, may be fully actualised by motherhood and may only use her work to add to that actualisation, by earning additional funds for child rearing, while another might need work outside her mothering task to affirm her own personhood.

Activity
Reflect on your own life or the life of someone you know intimately and try to identify a time when you or they were prevented from progression by psychological needs.

HERZBERG'S TWO-FACTOR THEORY OF MOTIVATION

The American theorist Herzberg developed an idea to explain what motivates workers and, although it incorporates existing theories, it has attracted a good deal of attention. Herzberg is a very charismatic figure. He called his theory the *two-factor theory of motivation*. His research was based on questionnaires and interviews.

He maintains that in any work situation, one can distinguish between the factors that dissatisfy and those that satisfy workers. The interesting thing is that these are not opposites of each other. Changing the dissatisfying factors does not turn them into satisfying or motivating factors.

Herzberg divided the elements which the people he questioned claimed motivated them into two groups. He claims that one set answers the question *'Why work harder?'* and the other set answers the question *'Why work here?'*.

Set 1: Motivational factors	Set 2: Maintenance factors
(Satisfiers)	(Dissatisfiers)
Recognition	Salary
Achievement	Conditions
Responsibility	Policies
Advancement	Inter-personal relationships
Q Why work harder?	*Q Why work here?*

Where Set 2 conditions obtain, there is a low staff turnover and low rate of absenteeism, as in the case given for the satisfaction theory (page 30).

Where Set 1 conditions obtain, there is a great deal of activity, new targets, fresh approaches, new developments and much excitement.

PSYCHOLOGICAL THEORY OF THE LOCUS OF CONTROL

This theory, originally described by Rotter (1966), provides a further motivator: the need human beings have to be in control of their own lives (Rubin and McNeil, 1983).

For some individuals, events in their lives are seen as 'bad luck' or 'good luck'. To become rich, you play the lottery. To get a good job, you need to know the right people. In other words, life events are attributable to external factors. This type of person is said to have an *external locus of control*.

Conversely, individuals with an *internal locus of control* attribute all events entirely to their own efforts or to their own shortcomings. They did not get the job because they gave a bad interview, they did not pass the exam because they did not study hard enough and so forth.

Those with an internal locus of control work harder and are more successful because everything is not left to luck, because luck does not play a significant part in their lives. One professional has noted that 'the harder I work, the luckier I get'.

It is useful for any manager to observe which staff have internal and which have external locus of control because the motivating techniques that can be applied in each case will vary.

> **Activity**
> Reflect on a team of people with whom you work closely. For each member of the team, ask yourself the following:
> - does he or she expect rewards from hard work?
> - does he or she expect rewards from luck factors?

Non-traditional theories of motivation

JOB ENHANCEMENT

Job enhancement (also known as job enrichment) is a technique used to make a job more interesting or rewarding to the worker, e.g. a nursery officer's job could be enriched or enhanced by being made responsible for student supervision or for NVQ assessing or for curriculum planning. Support in any of these roles would also need to be offered. However, it is more feasible to offer training and allocate 45 minutes supervision per week than to try and undertake all these tasks alone. This strategy also has the desirable effect of extending staff experience.

While the purpose of enhancement is to motivate the member of staff by making their job more interesting there is a spin-off benefit in that it is also a good method of delegating tasks and creating a forum for supervision.

QUALITY CIRCLES

A totally different approach to motivation is the idea of the *quality circle*, which was widely established in Japan before being adopted in America and Europe in the 1980s.

The fundamental nature of a quality circle is to motivate individuals through participation in decision making and reinforcement by positive feedback of results. It is of most benefit to organisations where quality performance is largely a function of individual effort and attention. The quality control methodology (which is almost a ritualistic approach in Japan) requires considerable effort to establish and sustain.

A quality circle meeting

Quality circles are widely used in manufacturing industries. A quality circle comprises a group of people – both managers and workers – in a single area or department within an organisation, which meets regularly to study ways of improving quality and to monitor progress towards such goals.

It is a participative device and quality circles are generally established on a voluntary basis. Those volunteering typically make up about half of the direct and indirect workers involved in the activities of a particular department. They may be offered training in the analysis and identification of quality problems and problem-solving procedures. Once any training is completed, the circle is formed and is invited to tackle particular quality problems either nominated by the management or identified by the circle itself. Each quality circle will normally tackle a series of projects, one at a time, identifying quality problems and means of eliminating such problems and establishing targets to be achieved through quality improvement

Wherever employed, the quality circle approach rests upon the motivation of individuals and the organisation's efforts to improve quality through error reduction. The technique could readily be adopted by nursery managers because small staff teams already exist in most nurseries. The work of the quality circles would readily facilitate the quality control procedures outlined in Chapter 4.

OPEN BOOK MANAGEMENT

This motivating notion was developed in an engineering company in Springfield, Massachusetts, USA, in the early 1990s. The leader of that 800 strong organisation, Jack Stack, devised a management system which started when he ran a two-day seminar explaining the minutiae of the business to all the staff. He saw business 'like a small game' and claimed you could not enjoy the game unless you understood the rules. He wanted his people to enjoy the game so he explained the rules.

The company (or representatives of the whole company) meet every two weeks to see the open account books and so understand the game. At least they know the score:

- they know how much is coming in – money and orders
- they know how much is going out – salaries and costs
- they know how what the bottom line is – the knowledge of a fall in profits brings out the 'E' factors, referred to earlier, without the need to resort to more complex methods.

Jack Stack states emphatically that the company has profit sharing and shared ownership but it is not a democracy. The leader makes the decisions. He claims that in terms of the history of staff motivation it is the obvious that everyone misses. The obvious is that when workers understand the rules they will play the game. It is dazzlingly simple if it works.

Activity
Consider the non-traditional theories of motivation:
- job enhancement
- quality circles
- open-book management.
Could any of these methods be applied to your nursery or centre? Write notes on how you could implement these methods.

Staff motivation is one of the most serious tasks of any manager.

Sometimes the best motivator is simply to roll up your sleeves and get stuck in. This is particularly effective if a really unsavoury task is involved. In this way you are motivating by example.

Sometimes – sadly – you can only resort to apply Herzberg's famous third factor of motivation which he calls K.I.T.A., standing for **k**ick **in**to **a**ction.

> I'm sure these have got a lot further away!

To fully motivate staff, a manager should give them confidence in their jobs – by explaining the context of the work, giving confidence in themselves by praising work well done and giving challenges, and giving confidence in the team by treating everyone equally and by using the creativity of the team when tackling problems. Good motivators also show concern for staff in times of trouble and provide good examples by their own behaviour.

Leadership theories

What makes a good leader and how someone can learn to be a good leader are immensely important questions for any manager. Can you be a 'born leader'? Not surprisingly, there have been a number of attempts to quantify and qualify the characteristics of leadership.

CHARISMATIC LEADERS

Before we look at 'ordinary' leaders it is helpful to dispose of the notion of *charismatic* or magical leadership. Some individuals are said to possess a magical power which causes others to follow them. There have only been a few in the whole of our history and in this context it is not helpful to think in magical terms except to exclude them.

Activity

In a group, brainstorm the names of people in history who you consider to have 'magical' powers of leadership – for good but also for evil.

When you are clear about charismatic power, it will be obvious that most leaders are made and not born leaders – even if sometimes they have some characteristics that help.

THE TRAIT APPROACH

This represents the first major approach to theorising in this area, and the broad aim was to determine those personal attributes that make a person a leader.

A number of characteristics have been proposed as being advantageous (at least in men) including height, weight, an attractive appearance, self-confidence, and being well-adjusted and intelligent.

However, several studies and reviews have demonstrated that the typical leader is only slightly more intelligent than the average member of the group. Most researchers discover that leaders are neither extremely authoritarian nor extremely egalitarian but somewhere in between. They are often taller (or very much shorter) than the group and do have an attractive appearance and self confidence.

THE SITUATIONAL APPROACH

This approach began to emerge in the 1950s and was an attempt to supplement and rectify some of the shortcomings of the traditional trait approach. For instance, the situational approach acknowledges that leadership involves leaders and followers in various role relationships and that there are several paths to becoming validated as a leader. This approach has been superseded by later theories.

THE CONTINGENCY MODEL OF LEADER EFFECTIVENESS

In the 1960s there was a revival of interest in the personality characteristics of leaders, but this was a much more sophisticated approach than the trait approach and one which also represented an extension of the situational approach.

A major figure in this new approach was F.E. Fielder whose contingency model (1972) for the analysis of leadership effectiveness is mainly concerned with the fit or match between a leader's personal qualities or leadership style, on the one hand, and the requirements of the situation, on the other.

Leadership style

Fielder saw style as either *task-oriented* or *relationship-oriented*.

He began by measuring the extent to which leaders distinguish between their most and least preferred co-worker (LPC) and developed a scale which gives an LPC score. This score determines whether a person is relationship-oriented or task-oriented.

■ Someone with a high LPC score still sees their least preferred co-worker in a relatively favourable light and also tends to be more accepting, permissive, considerate and person-oriented in relationships with group members (relationship-oriented).

■ By contrast, someone with a low LPC score sees their least-preferred co-worker very differently, regards them unfavourably, and also tends to be directive, controlling and dominant in relationships with group members (task-oriented).

Best fit

Fielder then investigated the fit between these two styles of leadership and the needs of the situation.

The hypothesis that he tested is that the effectiveness of a leader is contingent or dependent upon the fit between:

■ the leader's style – whether task-orientated or relationship-orientated
■ the quality of leader–member relationships
■ task structure
■ the position-power of the leader in the organisation.

The *quality of leader–member relationships* refers to the extent to which the leader has the confidence of the group and to the general psychological climate of the group.

Task structure refers to the complexity of the task and the number of possible solutions: the more unstructured the task, the more the leader must motivate and inspire members to find solutions themselves rather than relying on the back-up of their superiors or resorting to rules.

The *leader's position-power* refers to the power inherent in the role, e.g. the rewards and punishments at the leader's disposal and the organisational support for the leader from superiors.

From studies like this, theorists were able to conclude that when any individual is put into a position where a group of people has to depend on their efforts, they tend to accept the responsibility and the challenge. That is, they behave like leaders. Just as crucially, they are recognized as leaders by the rest of the group.

Compared with people occupying peripheral positions, leaders tend to:

■ send more messages
■ solve problems more quickly
■ make fewer errors, and
■ be more satisfied with their own and the group's efforts.

Fielder thinks leaders are made – not born.

ADDITIONAL CHARACTERISTICS OF THE LEADER

Two additional personal characteristics have been added to the trait theory in recent times.

One is that some leaders have the capacity to take an overview of a situation. The so-called 'helicopter view' means that they are aware of other factors that affect the work and are impinging on the situation. They *can* see the wood for the trees.

The second is the capacity to work with uncertainty, to, as Tom Peters (1982) puts it, 'roll with ambiguity'. This is the ability to continue functioning well without a clear idea of what might happen and what the next step might be. This capacity allows for great flexibility and encourages a healthy response to change. This capacity in a leader has always been desirable but is now practically essential.

ADDITIONAL ROLES OF THE LEADER

The leader of a team, a small group, or a large organisation acts as an *ambassador* for the team or the group or the organisation. It is the leader's job to project the feelings and needs of members, to communicate their value and to demonstrate that the team he or she leads is the best, the most cohesive, the hardest working and so forth. The level to which he or she can fulfill this function will be used by those inside and out as a measure of the leader's worth and also of the team's worth.

This is one of the most significant tasks of any manager because, as a bottom line, we all want to be on the winning side and in the winning team.

GOOD PRACTICE

Role model: as a leader or manager, staff will inevitably copy and emulate you. This is a sobering concept but must be borne in mind constantly in the child care setting because *as the staff are treated, so will they treat the children and from this modelling the children will be moulded.*

Although it is important to recognise that not anyone can fill any role, a helpful lesson from the theory for any nursery manager is that finding oneself in a position of leadership will bring out hidden talents. Certainly as far as research studies are concerned it seems to be the person's position in the network, and not their personality, which accounts for their success in the leadership role.

CASE STUDY

'I once knew a nursery where the true leader was the cook. She allowed the manager to do the administration, she allowed the staff to look after the children but she controlled both and was consulted on all issues – she held the power. I have also worked in a college where the true leader was the Senior Janitor – nothing happened without his approval.'

Activity

This activity is designed to develop self-analysis skills.

Mark yourself out of ten for each word in the following list of 'emotionally charged' terms used to describe leaders and managers:

EXTENSIVE EXPERIENCE

ABILITY

DYNAMIC, CREATIVE APPROACH

DEDICATED AND HARD WORKING

LOYAL

OUTSTANDING PLANNING AND ORGANISATION ABILITY

ENTHUSIASTIC WITH DRIVE

DRIVE

INITIATIVE

AMBITION

FULL COMMITMENT AND PROFESSIONALISM

MATURITY

SELF AWARENESS

ADAPTABILITY

HIGHLY MOTIVATED

SELF MOTIVATED

EXCELLENT COMMUNICATIONS SKILLS

ABILITY TO INFLUENCE

FLEXIBLE

ASSERTIVE

ADAPTABLE

GOOD INTERPERSONAL SKILLS

DISCREET

EFFECTIVE

KEYS TO GOOD PRACTICE

- Ensure you always respect staff as human beings.
- Be sure to praise good work.
- Ensure you always treat staff justly and equally.
- Be ready to join in with unsavoury tasks, or to stay late and demonstrate by example your own commitment to the work.
- Avoid rewarding poor performance.
- Avoid victimising or favouring individual members of staff
- Give staff individual time on a regular basis when they are undertaking difficult or new tasks, e.g.
  - supervising special needs children
  - supervising students
  - supervising curriculum development.

4 POLICIES AND PROCEDURES FOR QUALITY CARE

> ## What this chapter covers:
> - relevant parts of the 1989 Children Act and the role of the manager
> - the ethos of the nursery
> - mission and policy
> - total quality management (TQM)
> - using Policy Statements to write procedures and develop nursery routines

The aim of this chapter is to examine the effects of the 1989 Children Act and other legislation on the service and on the management role in child care.

The Children Act has been a great support to workers keen to deliver quality child care and has made explicit many of the practices which have long been considered desirable, e.g. working with parents as partners or allocating key workers or producing written policies.

In this chapter we suggest management strategies to bring in the policies recommended by the Act and considered desirable as good practice in the UK today. This chapter is about routines (procedures), what they are, where they come from and how they affect the manager's role in the child care service.

In addition we discuss total quality management (TQM), a management concept which claims that if things are written down and put into some sort of routine (systematised) then the quality of the work can be maintained throughout the ups and downs of everyday events and minor crises.

Here, again, there is no real research work from child care settings – although our own professional intelligence (and several sad incidents in the field) are testament to the fact that if routines are not observed and systems are not laid down, bad practice follows and the children suffer. It has not been the tradition to enforce TQM which is long overdue in an area where it could be a matter of life and death.

Relevant parts of the 1989 Children Act and the role of the manager

The relevant sections of the Act are Part II (Local Authority Support for Children) and Part X (Child Minding and Day Care for Young Children). The Act and all the associated regulations are very detailed.

GOOD PRACTICE

All nurseries should hold a copy of the relevant sections so that reference can be made to them at any time.

The regulations deal with private disputes between parents about children, court orders and care proceedings as well as with day care and fostering.

The primary aims are to protect children, to prevent family breakdown, and to ensure minimum standards in services for children and their families. As we have noted, many such services have to be registered and inspected by the local authority, including day care and childminding of the under-8s. The range of day care services for the under-8s is shown in the diagram below. The DFEE or the local authority is responsible for ensuring that acceptable standards are met in all of these.

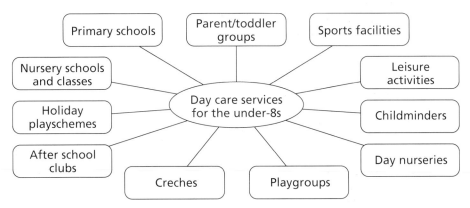

Day care services for under-8s

The key principles emphasised throughout the Children Act are outlined below.
- *The primary concern.* The welfare of children must be the prime concern of workers and authorities.
- *The role of parents.* Parents have *responsibilities* towards their children – they do not have absolute rights as if children were possessions (this was never explicitly stated until this Act).
- *Sharing care.* Workers and authorities should work in partnership with parents.
- *Children's individuality.* In the provision of services local authorities must take into account each child's and family's racial origin, religious persuasion and cultural and linguistic background (this is supported by the UN convention).
- *Disabilities.* Children with disabilities are specifically included within 'Children in need' as defined by the Act.

The sections most relevant to day care and the manager's role are published in the Guidance and Regulations, Volume 2, Chapters 4–9.

Part X Schedule 9 and 2 (Regulations and Guidance) of the Children Act places upon local authorities duties and powers to ensure minimum standards of care for young children and to assist in the development of standards. The local authority is required to keep a register and to inspect the premises of all persons who provide day care for children under eight within that area.

The local authority's duty is to ensure only the *minimum* standard and, although this term is not clearly defined, it is generally agreed to be a standard which will keep the children safe and comfortable.

There are loop holes in the regulations which can lead to bad practice and these are currently under review.

REGISTRATION OFFICER

To ensure the standards, the authority must carry out an annual inspection and the nursery/centre must meet the expense of this inspection. It is carried out by the official Registration Officer appointed for the purpose. Some authorities call these colleagues 'Day Care Advisers' to reflect a more developmental supportive and less inspectoral role. Whatever name they are given, their responsibility is to the authority, which has the duty to protect the children, and not to the nursery, however harmonious the relationship developed may be.

One of the side effects of the Children Act was the rapid increase in the staff in these posts in local authorities, often doubling or tripling over a two-year period, providing welcome career opportunities for qualified experienced nursery staff.

GOOD PRACTICE

It is useful to keep an updated file of the legislation for use with parents and staff, and to hold on file the names of experts who are available as a resource to answer questions or clarify issues should they arise.

The ethos of the nursery

The primary task of the manager is to create and control the ethos of the nursery. The dictionary definition of 'ethos' is 'the characteristic spirit or disposition of an organisation' and it closely resembles what theorists call culture (although 'ethos' is a more appropriate vocational term), which we dealt with in Chapter 2.

The ethos of any child care organisation can be measured by a range of performance indicators which tell us whether or not quality care is being provided for the children.

The ethos or the culture of a centre is palpable to all users and visitors. It is difficult to define but it is not difficult to identify even on the basis of a very few visits.

For this reason it is vital that the ethos, like the culture in theoretical terms, is appropriate to the task of the centre and reflects the published policies and declared mission statement.

GOOD PRACTICE

You will be able to form a good idea of whether any nursery/centre has a good ethos, if you ask the following questions.
- Are the children happy? (That is, are they engaged and functioning at their age-related developmental level, without undue noise, squabbling or minor injuries?)

- Does the environment ensure that every child is respected as an individual?
- Is the dignity and autonomy of the children respected?
- Does the environment promote enthusiasm for learning and skills acquisition?
- Does the environment encourage children to express themselves freely and to be spontaneous?
- Does the centre offer a stable learning and caring environment?
- Is self confidence promoted in the children?
- Does the centre promote good health?
- Does the centre encourage sociability and co-operation?
- Does the centre treat everyone equally, irrespective of gender, race, religion or disability?
- Is cultural diversity fully expressed?
- Is the centre fully sensitive to family influences?
- Is the centre in harmony with the wider community within which it is situated?

Each of the above questions can be answered by a policy or by a procedure or by the mission statement, which is dealt with in the next section.

In the nursery

Does the centre have a statement of aims and objectives which supports these values? Are there clear strategies for putting these objectives into practice? Does the organisation, work routines and activities programme reflect the aims, objectives and strategies of the centre? Do all the staff – trained and untrained – agree with and actively support these objectives?
See Sample 6, page 161.

Mission and policy

The nursery manager must articulate and record a mission statement, policy statements, procedures and other publicity material. The manager must create a team or group to share in the work of producing these documents.

THE MISSION STATEMENT

A sensible mission statement is useful to the parents and staff, and others involved in the centre, and is merely a succinct statement of the aims of the organisation. It is helpful to have the staff articulate exactly what the nursery is trying to do.

While such statements have been made by managers of many organisations for many years, it is only in very recent times – noticeably since the 1989 Act – that managers in child care have joined their number.

Here are some examples of mission statements for different organisations.

'Our mission is to contribute to the increased performance and competitive advantage of UK organisations by establishing, through the Investors in People Standard, the framework for effective investment in training and development for all people to meet business needs.'

Investors in People UK Limited

'The centre works to ensure that the educational and social needs of the children will be identified and provided for with due care and attention and in such a manner as will offer a reliable service for working parents, seeking wherever possible to enhance the quality of the children's total experience of family life.'

Anyplace Nursery Centre

'The Council will strive throughout its work to enable professional workers in children's care and education to gain access to training and assessment in order that they provide the highest quality service to children and families. The Council will also act as a focus for national standards in children's care and education.'

The Council for Awards in Children's Care and Education

An effective mission statement will:

- state clearly the purpose or intention of the organisation
- indicate an underlying value system
- be written in good and plain English
- be no less than 30 and no more than 100 words long
- be translated into the first languages of all of the users.

All workers in an organisation – particularly in a child care organisation – collectively own the philosophy contained in the mission Statement, and own the policies which are the distillation of the beliefs and intentions it contains. The group who write the statements must therefore have all staff, or representatives of all staff, involved. The group actually writing the statement should be between three and eight in number.

It is the role of the nursery manager to convene, facilitate, chair and steer this working group. It is the leader's task to establish policies and procedures for quality care.

The first meeting of the writing group will set the tone for the many that must follow, and should be handled carefully to ensure that it is relaxed and informal. Staff will not give of their best unless they feel valued and well supported. In preparing for the meeting, the manager should make some notes of ideas for the nursery's mission, for example:

'To care for and educate the children of the employees of the Anyplace Biscuit Company, to meet the needs of the children, to reflect the wishes and satisfy the child care needs of the parents and to facilitate the work of the Company.'

'To support mothers on drug rehabilitation programmes and assist them in the care of their children, offering training, guidance and support in the development of parenting skills for that purpose.'

Writing a mission statement

'To provide a structured educational environment for the care of children of Anyplace Hospital staff, respectful of their role in that organisation, in such a manner as to reflect their cultural diversity and allow for their flexible and unsocial work patterns.'

In the nursery

Provide samples of other mission statements for your writing group. Sample 1 (given on page 150) may be used or you could ask other nurseries. The local social services day care advisor will also be pleased to assist you with other examples.

Provide writing materials (flip charts and markers are ideal) and also refreshments.

Using the samples to hand the group should then brainstorm what they consider to be the mission of the organisation with which you are all involved and which you all know well even if it has never been articulated or recorded in quite this way before. It may help to brainstorm key words or phrases first, and then build these into ideas of the mission.

From the material thus generated, a statement can be assembled and checked against the above criteria to ensure that it has all the necessary features. The mission statement should be constructed in such a way that it will remain unchanged over time – it should be general – and not need adjusting.

The mission statement can be used on all of your publicity material, on the staff publicity and on the parents notice board.

See Sample 1, page 150.

POLICIES

The 1989 Children Act calls for *policies*. Policies exist to protect the children, the parents and the staff and to ensure that everyone using the centre is absolutely clear about the way the organisation functions and about what to do at all times.

A policy is 'a course of action or administration recommended or adopted by an organisation'. It is an articulated explanation of the way that a nursery will approach an area of work within it's culture. A policy is a collective agreed statement of beliefs.

There are four main policies demanded under the Children Act:

- Equal Opportunities Policy
- Parents as Partners Policy
- Health and Safety Policy
- Child Protection Policy.

Activity

This activity is designed to develop skills in identifying policies.

In groups:

- read the questions about the nursery listed on pages 46–47. Each question reflects one of the policies required by the Act.
- consider each question in turn and write down for each one the policy it refers to.

Examples of policies covering these areas can be found in Samples 2, 3, 4 and 5 on pages 151–160.

However, alongside these essential policies, the Act strongly recommends adopting other policies where they are appropriate and desirable for the well being of the nursery. Some common examples are:

Admissions Policy
Acceptable Behaviour Policy
Food Policy
Volunteer Policy
Key Worker Policy
Settling In Policy
Intimate Care Policy (staff protection)
Staffing Policy
Staff Training Policy
Fees Policy
Language Policy
Curriculum Policy
Child Collection Policy
Outings Policy
Quality Control Policy

Examples of such policies can be found in Samples 7–11, on pages 163–170.

(Note: Quality Control Policy is not required by the Act but provides a useful management strategy for systematising, monitoring and revisiting policies both demanded and voluntary.)

The nursery can add policies to reflect local needs or to identify a philosophy, e.g. for a special religious or ethnic group. Samples of standard formats for policies are given in Appendix A.

On first encounter the work of writing this material will seem very daunting to your group but assuming many samples are available and staff are empowered to voice their opinions the work will progress steadily. All of this work can be used as a focus for staff development

Keep all the finished work in a ring binder. Label it well and have a copy available in the staff room and in the office. Ask staff to sign their contributions and to include the experience on their CVs. This work will be greatly assisted if the National Children's Bureau Guidelines are used in conjunction with the Children Act as source material.

In the nursery

It is a good idea to meet regularly at the same time and place and to undertake the work in small bite sizes. Start with the mission statement and the legally required policies and move on to writing the procedures which reflect the policies. Use the samples provided in Appendix A as the basis for your work.

See Samples 1–5, 7–11 and 48–49 on pages 150–160, 163–170 and 221–223.

Total quality management (TQM)

Total quality management (TQM) is a management technique which was developed in the late 1970s in response to the gradual acceptance of the idea that – at least modest – change was becoming commonplace in most organisations. TQM was adopted as a theme in businesses, e.g. British Telecom in the early 1980s, to encourage continuous improvement in every aspect of the work of the organisation. TQM is based on the assumption that continual striving to reach higher and higher standards in every part of the organisation will provide a series of small improvements that will add up to superior performance. Such efforts point in the right direction, towards organisations able to learn and adapt to the needs of a rapidly changing environment. TQM does not entail dramatic changes in structure and systems – more of a continuous fine tune than a sudden and complete overhaul.

TQM can be brought into nurseries and child care settings using the structure of the Children Act, the policies it requires and the procedures developed from these.

From each one of the four policies required, procedures can be devised. A policy is a collective agreed statement of beliefs. Procedures are the practices by which the policies are implemented in the nursery – the way of doing things. The procedures are underpinned by the policies.

Using Policy Statements to write procedures and develop nursery routines

Each policy statement underpins a number of procedures, as illustrated in the diagrams below. For example, equal opportunities policy gives rise to procedures for admissions, staffing, training, curriculum planning, food and administration. These procedures, in turn, give rise to routines.

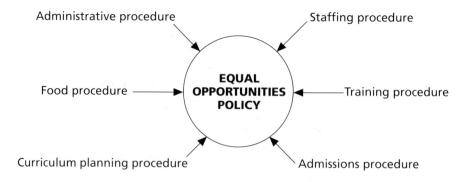

Procedures underpinned by equal opportunities policy

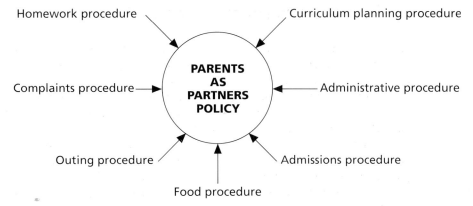

Procedures underpinned by parents as partners policy

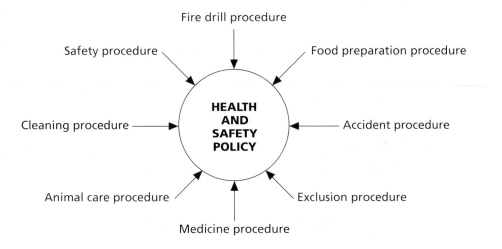

Procedures underpinned by health and safety policy

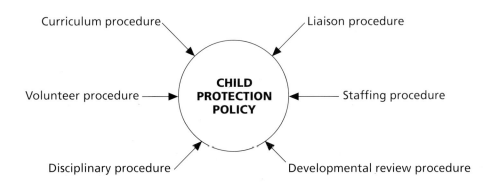

Procedures underpinned by child protection policy

In the nursery

This exercise can be undertaken for each policy as it is written. The result will be a portfolio of procedures which will provide a system of articulating and maintaining the standards in the centre and among the staff.

See Samples 12–18 inclusive, on pages 171–178.

If it is agreed to adopt a policy on quality control, this allows the development of a quality assurance system which will technically liberate the manager from constant checking up and will allow more time for the art of management.

This same quality control technique can be used for all functions, vocational and administrative, e.g. to check off staff appraisals.

The policies, procedures and routines should be stored in a ring binder to allow for daily, weekly or monthly checking. A tick list or signature system can be introduced so that a system of monitoring the work is built into the nursery routines. This means that when you come to evaluate the processes and check the systems, there is already an existing structure – a routine.

In the nursery

To evaluate the effectiveness of the service, both in achieving its original aims and in the quality of the service provided, a mechanism can be developed for use by the manager and staff. Using the policies, procedures and routines, a list of performance indicators can be identified.

See Sample 30, page 192.

The standard work in this field has been undertaken by the National Children's Bureau, which has produced an invaluable guide indicating good quality child care. This work can be used to provide simple guidelines so that each facility evaluates the quality of its service against a common set of criteria.

This would also help users in choosing the child care appropriate to their needs, since it is currently difficult for the lay person to compare the quality of one nursery to that of another.

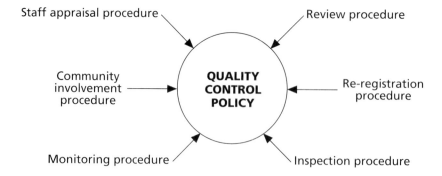

Procedures underpinned by quality control policy

An understanding of what quality means helps the manager to regulate the quality of care provided and monitor the training given to care givers.

There are opportunities in this area for staff development and for job enhancement.

Procedures to guard the staff

The policy on Intimate Care has been devised to underpin the procedures for the toiletry and intimate care delivered to children. It is a form of staff protection.

KEYS TO GOOD PRACTICE

- Ensure that you and all your staff are aware of the requirements of the 1989 Children Act. A pocket-sized volume covering all relevant areas is readily available and could be included in the staff induction programme.
- Make a copy of the questions on pages 46 and 47 (taken from the European discussion document on quality) and ask yourself these questions with respect to each child attending your nursery.
- Ensure that the nursery has, as a minimum, the four policies required under the Act written down and displayed.
- Ensure that the nursery meets the other legal requirements which demand written displayed items, e.g. fire drill.

---

5 SYSTEMS FOR ADMINISTRATION IN QUALITY CHILD CARE

> **What this chapter covers:**
> - administrative systems for managing the children's records
> - a system for nursery administration
> - use of technology
> - marketing the nursery
> - systems for ensuring excellence

This chapter is about the sort of routine tasks which in themselves seem very boring but without which the nursery cannot function. The areas discussed in this chapter would come into the science side of the great management divide between 'the science' and 'the art' of management.

It is vital to make administrative systems work in support of the child care services and not in opposition to them. The routines set up should improve the care given to the children and not be at its expense, either because the administrative work takes staff away from the children or becomes overly bureaucratic (in the negative sense of that word) and stress inducing.

However, it is true to say that the administration has to be done – the fees collected, the salaries processed, the rotas devised, the bills paid, and so forth. The skills needed in this area must be acquired. It is a bit like the Highway Code – you might find it tedious to learn but you will not be successful unless you do.

Administrative systems for managing the children's records

Every day care centre needs systems for records which must be kept under the Children Act. Such records must be available for inspection by the local authority at any time. These are changing working documents and all staff should have access to and be familiar with them.

REGISTERING THE CHILDREN

A procedure for registering the children must be set up and records of the following kept:
- full name, address and date of birth of each child attending or being looked after on the premises (hold in card index and child's individual file)
- names of the parents/carers, home and work telephone numbers (hold in card index and child's individual file); some centres also ask for photographs
- an emergency contact number and details of the emergency contact person (if

different from above) and any other person authorised to collect the child (hold in card index and child's individual file); some centres also ask for photographs

- information about the religion, ethnic origin, culture and language(s) spoken, if the parent/carer is prepared to provide this (policy available, procedure recorded and on child's individual file)
- information about any health problems or other special requirements, e.g. diet, that the child may have (hold in card index and child's individual file). Display dietary requirements in kitchen
- name address and telephone number of family doctor and health visitor (hold in card index and child's individual file)
- consent form for outings and car journeys, to be held in child's individual file
- consent form for the administration of medication (see Sample 31), to be held in child's individual file
- a record of any medicine administered to the child, to be held in child's individual file.

In the nursery

It is both practical and sensible to devise standing forms for use in the day-to-day affairs. Forms for parental permission should be devised using the samples provided as models. A standard package of permission/approval forms should be kept in a neat file and these discussed with parents when each child is admitted into the nursery. It is important that parents understand the implications of their signature.

See Samples 21, 31, 32 and 33, pages 181–182 and 193–195.

Other records that should be kept are:
- a daily record of attendance and discharge (policy available and procedure recorded)
- a record of child protection concerns (policy available and procedure recorded)
- an accident/incident book (procedure recorded and in child's individual file)
- a record of the food served every day (policy available and procedure recorded). Menu displayed
- a record of fire drills and safety checks (procedure recorded)
- names and addresses of staff, assistants and key suppliers (on file)
- in the case of centres which are day care providers, names and contact details of the board of directors and management committee or group (on file).

A system for nursery administration

In the administration of a nursery four simple basic systems are required, as detailed below.
1. A card index system:
   - for the children's details
   - general, for suppliers and emergency services.

2. A filing system:
   - for children's records
   - for staff records
   - for the premises
   - for budgets/accounts and financial planning
   - for forward planning.
3. A display system
   This is necessary because much of the work must be displayed to meet the needs and in the spirit of the Children Act.
4. A book system
   Various books are also needed:
   - minor accident book
   - accident and emergency book
   - duty rota book
   - log book (for recording day to day events)
   - petty cash book
   - incident book
   - fire drill book.

CARD INDEX SYSTEM

Children's details

This box should be stored by the telephone and should contain a card for each child with the contacts to be used in the event of illness or other emergency.

General

This box should also be stored by the telephone and should contain emergency numbers for plumbers, electricians, non-999 police, staff home numbers, i.e. numbers for any emergencies not connected to individual children.

It is perfectly possible to keep these indexes in the same box if space allows and there is no issue of confidentiality, e.g. in the case of sharing an office with another facility.

Card index systems are only useful if they are kept up-to-date and all details are recorded on the cards themselves and not on messy notes or post-it stickers. The responsibility for the card index should be structured into the manager's workload or delegated to a member of staff.

FILING SYSTEM

Children's records

Records for each individual child must be kept under the Children Act. These should include a developmental progress record (see Sample 34) for the child to proceed with him or her to school.

Staff records

Individual files should hold:
- application form

- references
- record of sending police check (the actual police check form is retained by, and is the property of, the registering authority)
- salary details and increments
- holiday and absentee records (can be held in this file or in a card index depending on the size and complexity of the organisation)
- copies of appraisal forms, or records of when appraisals happened if the policy is not to record appraisals
- records of any courses taken as in-service training or at the expense of the employer
- records of any written warnings which may have been issued.

The general staffing file will hold:
- advertising for staff – records of previous advertisements, advertisement artwork and so forth
- sample job descriptions/person specifications
- blank police check forms
- health check forms
- staff development file, including details of courses offered locally.

Budgets/accounts and financial planning

For small nurseries a simple double-entry book keeping system will suffice for records of income and expenditure (see Sample 20, page 180). The important thing is to monitor the cash flow: invoice the parents on time (see Sample 23, page 185) and keep a careful check that they pay within the specified period. Encourage a culture of prompt settlement of accounts. Sample 19 (page 179) outlines financial procedures and can be adapted to fit your own situation.

Records of income can be used to work out anticipated income from occupancy rate prediction. Occupancy rate prediction is undertaken by a forward booking system and can be accurate for one month only (or whatever period is paid for in advance). An occupancy chart should be completed to predict the income and highlight the vacancies.

Activity

This activity is designed to develop skills in budgeting

1. Construct a sample budget based on a nursery or day care centre you know.
2. Examine the budget critically.
3. Suggest any improvements.

Using a planning programme allows income prediction. It also demonstrates that full-time children make prediction simple. So from a business point of view, full-time children make more sense. However, any empty slot is undesirable because it indicates a lost earning opportunity. Vacancies can be compensated for if savings are made on staff, e.g. if the nursery is not busy on one particular day it may be possible to use that time as off-duty for staff or to balance the use of part-time colleagues.

For example, an applicant wants a space for an under-2 child on Monday, when six children are already booked in. If you accept the booking for Monday this means an additional member of staff must be employed on that day. It is therefore in your interest to suggest Tuesday instead, as eight children are booked for Tuesday and three staff must be employed anyway as the number of children already exceeds six.

COSTING THE SERVICES

It is important when costing your services that you take account of the fact that parents will not wish to pay for holidays, whether bank holidays or summer holidays. However, you must still pay the staff, the rates, and all the other expenses. In calculating the fees you must take this into account.

Therefore if your fees (to cover all costs and meet all the nursery objectives) are to be £20.00 per day, the following equation should be used:

$$£20.00 \text{ per day} \times 365 = \frac{7300}{343} = £21.28$$

By dividing by 343, you are compensating for 8 days bank holiday and for 14 days annual holiday. Therefore, the true price per day you would charge is £21.50. Since the mornings tend to be more popular with parents the suggestion is that the morning charge is £11.50 and the afternoon £10.00, although this will vary with local conditions and many other factors.

FORWARD PLANNING

Plan occupancy as far ahead as possible – at least 3 months in advance. You can use computer programmes or a standard pro-forma to manage the waiting list. Suggest attendance alternatives to parents where it will help to balance the occupancy.

The system for forward bookings is vital.

GOOD PRACTICE

Time must be set aside each week to analyse the loading on the nursery balanced against the staffing and other costs. Steps should be taken to reduce staffing levels if the fees do not justify the expenditure, e.g. by employing part-time staff.

A system should be devised to facilitate forward planning and to estimate loading on spaces.

PLANNING EVENTS

An annual calendar can be drawn up to include:

- religious festivals
- children's vacations
- staff vacations
- seasonal outings
- nursery to school transitions creating spaces
- advertising for children's vacancies
- curriculum planning.

DISPLAY SYSTEM

Materials which must be displayed are:

- weekly menus
- fire exits
- fire drill procedure
- food allergy notices for individual children in the kitchen
- skin allergy notices for individual children in the bathroom
- daily events board – for staff communication.

GOOD PRACTICE

It is simple to devise work plans and display these in the nursery to facilitate routine tasks.

In the nursery

Sample 28 gives a standard list of displayed information. It is important that the manager reviews these displays regularly as they can easily deteriorate and create a poor image. This task can either be structured into the manager's week or delegated as part of a job enhancement.

See Sample 28, page 190.

(Note: these displays are in addition to normal vocational displays, e.g. parent's notice board, work displays etc.)

BOOKS SYSTEMS

Books, such as the incident book, should be kept in the office and treated with respect.

Whether any entries are made or not, the book should be signed off each week at a time arranged and noted.

The books themselves are simple. They require only the date and time, an entry and signature and, of course, the checking signature. For example:

13 October 1995   Fire Alarms Tested   Signed: *Jackie Sadek*
10.00 a.m.   Found in good order   Checked: *Elizabeth Sadek*

ROTA

If staff work in shifts, a formula for cover will need to be agreed. It is important to remember that it is not necessary for the staff to work the same times each day. It is empowering for staff to jointly arrange their own rota and this task can be safely delegated to them – although periodic checks should be made to ensure equity.

GOOD PRACTICE

It will develop trust among staff if they feel they are allowed to allocate duty times to fit in with their family commitments.

Use of technology

Another challenge for nursery managers is the use of technology to process and transmit information. A number of software packages have been developed for nursery management and these can be run on standard personal computers. There are several excellent packages for staff who feel confident with computers. These programmes may prove helpful once there are over 20 children; below that number a manual system is as easy to manage – unless the computer can be used for other nursery activities.

Whilst computers are always useful in any organisation which is subject to constant change (see also Chapter 9), a computer becomes *essential* if, and only if, it will perform one or more of the following functions for you:

■ increase the efficiency of the organisation (and so reduce the costs)
■ improve the quality (and perhaps the quantity) of the service
■ give staff more control over the work load.

Many nursery managers have found that computers are worthwhile and today many benefit from at least a rudimentary computer, but they are by no means necessary to run an efficient and top quality child care service. As a high expenditure item, it is a good idea to consider carefully before choosing to purchase a computer.

Remember also the GIGO effect: 'Garbage in, garbage out'. It is wholly unwise to put anything onto computer unless the manual version is already working well and is fully understood by the personnel involved.

If you are seriously considering making the transition from a paper-based system to software, the best advice is to write down and be clear in your own mind about exactly what you want the programme to *do for you*. Sample 27 (page 189) shows the type of records that might be kept on computer. Once you have written your ideas down, go along to nurseries in the area where appropriate software is in use and have it demonstrated. Only then can you make an informed decision.

If the computer takes staff away from the children then it is not a good investment.

Marketing the nursery

As we have already noted, it is important to keep the nursery places fully occupied.

In one local authority recently, information was sought on how parents had heard of day care services for under-8s. The breakdown of responses was as follows:

Friends	2262	Yellow pages	9
Local school	1300	Leaflets	8
Neighbours	914	Notices	8
Health visitor	642	Childminder	7
Public library	538	Word of mouth	7
Family member	401	Phoning	5
Social services department	252	Shop ads	5
Education department	171	Nursery itself	4
Newspapers	110	Parish magazines	4
National Childbirth Trust (NCT)	30	Work	4
Sports centres	23	Parent and toddler group	2
Borough/district councils	16	Community care	2
Childminder's group	14	Playgroup	2
Church	13	Other	10
Doctor's surgery	10		

If the response to the research is to be taken seriously then marketing should be designed accordingly.

GOOD PRACTICE

Care should be taken with the marketing budget as it can be an extremely expensive item. The research indicates that simply buying newspaper advertising space is not effective. Nothing replaces personal recommendation. Local service providers, school teachers and health visitors are always happy to recommend quality provision and strong links should be forged with these professionals.

Fashion among parents will have some effect on the marketing techniques to be used. It is undoubtedly true that partners are making more and more demands on nurseries to 'educate' the pre-school child. This is what the Americans call the 'pushdown' effect. Academic expectations are being pushed down the age groups so that demands for achievements once made on adolescents are now being made on younger children. In this the parents are supported by the Schools' Curriculum Assessment Authority who publish the pre-school curriculum.

The research indicates that the quality of the service is the single most important selling point as most recommendation come from existing users. Parents are – quite rightly – not ready to trust advertisements in this vital area.

Systems for ensuring excellence

The 'pursuit of excellence' was the main concern of managers in the 1980s and early 1990s. The movement was led on a popular level by Tom Peters, a charismatic American theorist.

Peters' work (1982) was based on case studies of the twelve most successful companies in the USA. He wanted to know why they were successful and he discovered that each of them were led by people who:

■ really understood the vocational aspects of their work (he quotes McDonalds where the leader genuinely could see beauty in a sesame seed bun)

■ were chasing quality and

■ remained close to the product.

He noted from his observations that these managers spent nearly all their time 'at the coal face' – in the car showroom, the hamburger restaurant or, in our case, the nursery. Peters called this 'managing by walking about'. In the evaluation or monitoring of work it helps if a system is in place against which standards can be measured while you walk about. If these monitoring systems tell you things which surprise you then you are not walking about enough.

Tom Peters

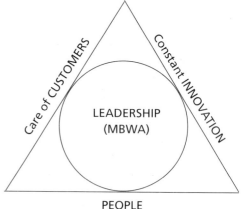

Care of CUSTOMERS · Constant INNOVATION

LEADERSHIP (MBWA)

PEOPLE

The MBWA triangle

For this process the policies and procedures assembled in the nursery portfolio, as discussed in Chapter 4, can be used.

Activity

This activity is designed to develop skills in monitoring and evaluating equipment. An equipment list from one nursery is given on page 65. Make a similar list for your nursery or adapt this list. Check all equipment for damage and dangerous wear and tear, for number of items and for cleanliness.

EQUIPMENT LIST

1	Guinea Pig Hutch	10	Storage Containers
1	Fireman's Hat	2	Wooden Climbing Frames
1	Builders Hat	5	Wooden Climbing Frame Platforms
1	Hockey Stick		
1	Plastic Spinning Top	1	Wooden Climbing Frame Ladder and Slide
2	Space Hoppers		
1	Elementary School Bus	1	Wooden Baby Crib
1	BMX (Bike with stabilisers)	3	Storage Containers
1	Little Tykes Plastic Climbing Frame with Slide	4	Slides (with Climbing Frame)
		2	Paddling Pools
1	Wooden Buggy	1	See-Saw
2	Metal Buggies	1	Shop
1	Car	1	Sand and Water Tray
1	Little Tykes Car	2	Child's Tables
1	Wooden Rocking Horse	2	Bean Bags
1	Go-Cart	20	Wooden Blocks
1	Bike with pedals	2	Metal Steps to Climbing Frame
1	Large Bike without pedals	3	Bats
1	Small Bike without pedals	1	Hose
1	Sport Bike	4	Brooms
1	Scooter	2	Gardening Forks
1	Wooden Rocking Horse	1	Spade
4	Safety mats	2	Rakes
1	Trampoline	1	Sack Shredded Paper (animals)
8	Hoops (large)	1	Ironing Board
7	Balls (large)	1	Step Ladder
7	Balls (medium)	4 ×	25 kg Sand
9	Balls (small)	1	Tunnel (blue)
9	Skipping Ropes	1	Leaflet Rack
8	Rubber Hoops (small)	1	Wooden Block Holder
19	Bean Bags	3	Wooden Chairs

PERFORMANCE INDICATORS

Performance indicators are numerically expressed relationships between one set of data and another which have been identified as a measure of the success, or absence of success, in an organisation, section or unit of an organisation.

They indicate relationships between:

(a) *resources and productivity*, e.g.

- number of cleaning hours required to keep a nursery to a targeted standard of cleanliness each week
- number of children being fed each day by a nursery kitchen
- number of hours lost to a staff team from illness, lateness etc.

- through-put of a nursery class.

(b) *two or more resources*, e.g.
- full and part-time staff
- trained and untrained staff
- professional and support staff.

(c) *two or more outcomes*, e.g.
- percentage attendance at day nursery by age, gender, racial origin.

(d) *productivity and potential market*, e.g.
- percentage of children from outside London attending Great Ormond Street Hospital.

Performance indicators are based upon two sets of comparisons:

(a) comparison of relationship between two or more factors (see above)
(b) comparison between:
- performance indicators in one centre over time
- performance indicators and externally or internally set targets, and
- performance indicators between two or more centres, e.g. percentage of staff illness in centre A compared with centre B over the same time period.

For any of these comparisons, the use of *only one* indicator will distort the result. Consider the examples given above and identify the other indicators necessary to reduce distortion. For example, the relative employment of full and part-time staff may depend more upon the number of appropriately trained people applying for employment within these categories than perseverance with policy targets.

Unfortunately, the media and authorities often focus upon single indicators and base judgements and planning or resource decisions upon them. These are then likely to be inaccurate, or even unjust. Education of lay and/or district authorities may be required to reduce oversimplification and misinterpretation. *It is necessary to understand that indicators indicate; they do not direct.*

Origin of requirements

Requirements for performance indicators often come from outside the organisation, usually from resourcing authorities. There may be a chain of requirements: national requiring regional; regional requiring local; local requiring them from organisations and so on.

They may also be used for internal reviewing and evaluation, resource deployment and quality assurance. 'There is a strong argument for small nurseries to set their own performance indicators and then to discuss these within their small teams or resource authorities, rather than, or as well as, waiting until figures are requested.

There is evidence to show that where indicators are designed, and 'owned' by people at operational levels, they are likely to be more accurate and less resented.

Quality of information

The 'garbage in, garbage out' principle applies, i.e. the aid to judgement these indicators provide depends upon the employment of accurate and reliable information. Where indicators are required by an external and higher authority, those who prepare them may fudge them in order to:

- defend their jobs, organisation, resources, status, reputation and/or

■ present a case for more resources.

Information inputs may also be unreliable because:

■ they are not considered by staff to be of sufficiently high priority, compared with 'getting on with the job'
■ they are required of professionals who resent this intrusion upon their perception of their specialist roles
■ they are obtained from people who are too distant from the activity being measured and therefore can misinterpret data
■ there is no mechanism for checking mistakes.

Collection cycles and time lag

Collection of complex data may take a considerable length of time. Data may also be completed at the end of the exercise, or time period, e.g. a financial year. If this is so, the aid performance indicators can offer to planning and resource decision making is limited by changes that may have taken place during the time lag, e.g. where decisions for the year 95/96 are based upon 93/94 indicators, as those for 94/95 are still being processed.

Shorter collection cycles are therefore recommended. These offer opportunities for speedier corrective or regulating action but by their frequency, probably cost more.

Cost of performance indicators

Recording, collecting and processing information for performance indicators involves resource costs. Opponents of their use argue that cost of their production may equal the resource savings resulting from more informed decisions.

Means are available to reduce cost, such as:

■ sampling, i.e. collection of information from representative examples
■ computerising the processing, which should also reduce the time lag
■ integrating the recording with routine activities, which is the system recommended in a child care context.

Hard and soft indicators

Hard performance indicators are based upon comparatively objective information, e.g. number of people resident in an institution over a year; average stay in a postnatal ward.

Soft performance indicators attempt to measure less quantifiable and/or more subjective factors, e.g. public reputation and quality of service. This cannot be measured in the same way as hard indicators and usually relies upon client/customer judgement, often using interviews or questionnaires. A 'harder' ingredient can be introduced in measuring such success factors, e.g. by recording the number of people recommended by friends, and the amount of repeat business. Soft indicators should not – for all their difficulties – be neglected; it can be argued that their significance to decision makers in judging the successful performance of an organisation equals that provided by hard indicators.

SWOT ANALYSIS

Another useful method of assessing a situation is a technique known as SWOT analysis. This technique is often used at times of change when contemplating expansion or contraction or before embarking on a marketing exercise or some other large expenditure.

   In brief, the idea is to consider the **S**trengths and **W**eaknesses of the internal organisation and compare these with the **O**pportunities and **T**hreats to the organisation from outside.

Strengths: internal factors likely to enhance performance, e.g. well-trained staff, a good location, good contacts with local schools.

Weaknesses: internal factors likely to hold back performance, e.g. high fixed costs, long-term staff illness.

Opportunities: external factors which could favour the organisation, e.g. introduction of pre-school voucher funding, a new housing development nearby.

Threats: external factors which could be detrimental to the organisation, e.g. the opening of a work-based nursery nearby taking children who were formerly regular attenders.

   Although this type of analysis is usually undertaken by management groups, it can be used to good effect in the nursery staff team as the basis for a focused discussion.

STRATEGIC PLANNING

The systems for budgeting and planning work that have been considered in this chapter are one part of the overall plan of the nursery. They take into account those aspects of the organisation that are quantifiable.

   There is another term borrowed from management theory, which describes a level of planning in which most successful business engage, called *strategic planning*. *Strategy* refers to a system of objectives and plans, as well as the allocation of resources to achieve these objectives and plans.

Financial planning is one part of the process of allocation of resources designed to achieve the organisation's objectives.

Strategic planning takes into account factors other than the financial, some of which are non-quantifiable and some of which are judgemental in character.

To be acceptable to the nursery, a decision not only has to be affordable, it has to fit in with the strategic plan of the organisation. In business, continued existence is the ultimate objective – the organisation has to plan to achieve this as it is engaged in fierce competition both for markets and resources. The strategic plan has to take into account the objectives of the organisation, some of which are expressed in terms of financial return or in market growth. The plan is based on a careful analysis of the relative strengths and weaknesses of the organisation, and an assessment of the opportunities in the markets open to it.

The strategic plan has to be based on more than the access to and control of financial resources. Personnel, supplies, market opportunities and technological change all have to be considered. Indeed, the organisation may also have social and psychological objectives that have to be taken into account.

The typical strategic plan sets out where it sees the organisation going over the next ten years or so. In which areas will it expand, in which will it contract? What growth target has it set itself? Will it rely on internal growth or will it resort to growth through acquisition? Which parts of the company will be sold off? The plan has to satisfy the financial objectives, the marketing objectives, and the social objectives of those making the decisions on behalf of the company.

There are many techniques that have been designed to assist companies in their strategic planning. One of the earliest of these was that developed and marketed by the Boston Consulting Group (1979). Their approach was to classify each area of the business on the basis of its relative market and technological competitiveness and the potential growth rate of that part of the business. Each area of the business, each segment, was classified as either a 'star', a 'dog', a 'cash flow' or a 'question mark'.

These classifications would be important when it came to making investment decisions. An investment proposal from a division classified as a 'dog' would be most unlikely to receive approval, this being an area of the business in which competitively one was at a disadvantage and an area with little or no market growth possibilities. However, an investment proposed by a division in the 'star' category would stand a good chance of being approved. The investment would have satisfied the question 'Does it fit in with the strategic plan?' It would, of course, still be necessary for the particular investment to satisfy the financial hurdle, e.g. to show a positive net present value.

Many other strategic planning techniques have been developed, one being that of the consulting group Organisation. This, as with the Boston Group approach, recognises that in a large and organisationally complex company, the resource allocation process will need to be in two stages. One is the formation of plans leading to the provisional allocation of capital at group level. The second is the approval of individual investment decisions. This section of the chapter is emphasising the first of these stages: there is more to capital investment appraisal than selecting between a number of unrelated investment proposals.

The Organisation approach is to divide a business into what are called strategic business units. It is to these units that the headquarters of the company will allocate investment funds. The units are analysed and placed into categories on the basis of their market attractiveness and their competitive strengths in these markets, a not dissimilar approach to that of the Boston Group.

CASE STUDY

A private pre-prep school, in an attempt to improve it's falling rolls when it changed hands, had it's whole future secured by taking two steps:
1. Opening a pre-nursery group for 2–3 year olds (who then stayed on to 13 years)
2. Opening an out of school care service before and after school each day and providing holiday cover.

By these two strategies, the school became a possible child care solution for working parents.

The new head met a local need and he also saved his school!

Planning can be divided into two types: top-down planning and bottom-up planning. Basically, strategic planning is top-down planning, but it should be a process which takes into account the views of the units being planned. The overall capital budget of a company must be based on strategic considerations; it cannot just be a selection of individual investment proposals that have come forward from the 'bottom up'. The capital investment plan of a company is part of a larger planning exercise.

PLANNING AND OBJECTIVES

The first stage in setting up any child care project is to establish its main objective(s) in line with policies and procedures, as discussed in Chapter 4. For example, this might be 'to provide quality child care at an affordable price'. The objectives are the starting point for project planning as they provide the lead for subsequent policy decisions, such as who the potential users of the facility will be, the ages of the children, the criteria for admission and so on. The objectives may be social or economic and, where the operation is set up as a separate legal entity, these will form a key part of the constitution. It is vital that they are clear, unambiguous statements and are fully agreed by the management team. Clear directives at an early stage may avoid crisis management situations occurring at the operational stage of the project.

It is likely that the parents/carers (as potential users) will be involved during these initial planning stages, indeed in the case of a work-based or community nursery they may be members of the steering committee. Incorporating their views early on will ensure that the future service provided will reflect their needs. A survey of potential users may be required at this point to assess their needs accurately. Provision should be made in the management structure to allow all users to have access to information, to participate in meetings and to have a forum for expressing their views on the service provided, once the project is up and running, as required under the Children Act.

The involvement of the users is important to the success of the project, as it is essential that the child care provision reflects and responds to the needs of the child and of the parent/carer. Child care should not be regarded in isolation from the family, home and culture. Quality child care provision can play an important role in the development of the child and therefore the parent/carer will need to be consulted about the type of service being provided.

KEYS TO GOOD PRACTICE

- Involve parents in the decision making processes of the nursery.
- Devise an annual programme for marketing the nursery.
- Set up and systemise administrative systems in accordance with the needs of the Children Act.
- Keep a card index with details of information which might be needed quickly by the telephone.
- In the event of an accident, record it in the proper manner and ask the parent/carer to sign to acknowledge that they have been notified of the accident.
- Ensure that a copy of the local authority procedures for child protection is available for staff use.
- Ensure that display items are in good order and that the care of such items are systematised.
- Develop procedures to measure the performance of the nursery.

6 *MANAGING THE CURRICULUM*

> ## What this chapter covers:
> - the manager's role in curriculum delivery
> - management strategies for planning the curriculum
> - the Schools Council Assessment Authority (SCAA) and implications for the manager's role

This chapter is about managing the curriculum – with a heavy emphasis on managing. It would be presumptive to suggest details of the curriculum in the light of the many learned works on the subject already on the market – see the list of references in Appendix B. However, strategies to bring in the curriculum are a neglected area and it is on that aspect that this chapter will concentrate.

The manager's role in curriculum delivery

The role of the manager in a child care setting in relation to the curriculum is to:
- ensure that the children are given a quality service, which includes an early years' curriculum
- consult and respect the wishes of the parents/carers, who are becoming more demanding in terms of appropriate curriculum input
- support and supervise the staff who give this service and deliver the curriculum
- provide adequate resources to enable the curriculum to function well
- set up a rich and stimulating environment in which the aims and principles of early childhood education can be delivered.

GOOD PRACTICE

To have an appropriate curriculum is the essence of quality care. It is the manager's role to plan, implement and evaluate this process, working closely with the nursery team.

In arranging this pre-school curriculum, staff will expect to provide for the development of the whole child for each individual child and will expect to maximise the child's potential in accordance with the underlying principles of early years' education.

AIMS AND PRINCIPLES OF EARLY CHILDHOOD EDUCATION

The aims of early childhood education are concerned with the development of the young child and are founded in the belief that:

- every child is a unique individual
- all children have skills and abilities that need to be brought out and built upon
- what they can do (not what they cannot do) should be the starting point in their education
- children have the right to develop physically, socially, emotionally, morally and intellectually to their full potential
- all children pass through the same processes of development even if not all at the same pace
- children learn through first hand experience, using their fives senses to develop an understanding of the world
- learning is holistic for young children and does not come under subject headings
- children need opportunity and space to explore their environment
- play is central to the child's learning process: 'Play is a child's work'.

Children have a natural desire to learn and it is through playing with real objects and materials that they begin to make sense of their world. The importance of play should always be respected in the devising of the nursery curriculum.

INFLUENCES ON CURRICULUM CHOICE

As already noted it is the manager's responsibility to plan, implement and review the curriculum. However, the choice or control of the philosophy underpinning the curriculum on offer will depend very much on the conditions in which the nursery is run, who owns it, who governs it and so forth.

In UK mainstream nursery school education it is usual to find a curriculum based on the teachings of Froebel (1782–1852), a German early years pioneer who advocated an informal structure, and who first noticed that 'Play is a child's work'.

Froebel's approach provided a fertile backdrop for those who followed, who adopted and adapted his teachings – Margaret McMillan and Susan Isaacs being perhaps the most famous. It is on the work of these educators that the mainstream early years curriculum is now based. The informal structure lent itself well to the changing needs of our educational system.

Froebel allowed great flexibility and the children's active planning, doing and reviewing advocated by the Highscope researchers in America was readily compatible with the public sector schools curriculum and has become widely used since it was first introduced in the late sixties and seventies to the UK.

In America both researchers and politicians were very encouraged by the long-term development of the needy children involved in their sample program and are loud in praise of the approach (Berrueta-Clement, J.R. and others, *Changed Lives: The Effects of the Perry Pre-School Program on Youths Through Age 19*, Highscope Press, 1984).

Interesting to note that both Maria Montessori and Rudolf Steiner in their times

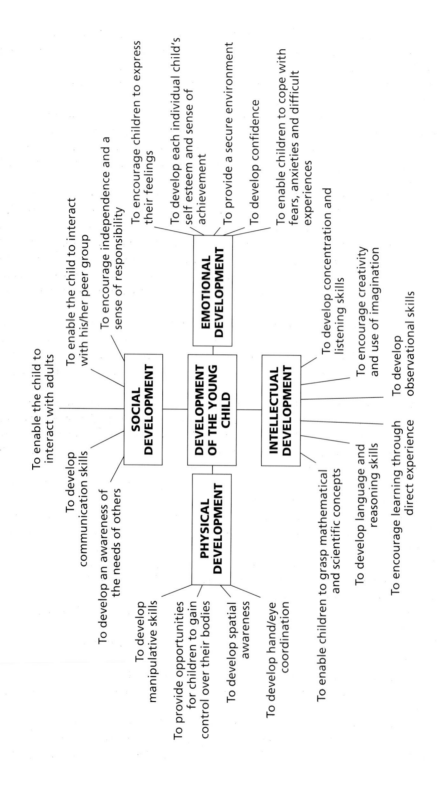

Aims of nursery education

DEVELOPMENT OF THE YOUNG CHILD

SOCIAL DEVELOPMENT
- To enable the child to interact with adults
- To enable the child to interact with his/her peer group
- To encourage independence and a sense of responsibility
- To develop communication skills
- To develop an awareness of the needs of others

EMOTIONAL DEVELOPMENT
- To encourage children to express their feelings
- To develop each individual child's self esteem and sense of achievement
- To provide a secure environment
- To develop confidence
- To enable children to cope with fears, anxieties and difficult experiences

PHYSICAL DEVELOPMENT
- To develop manipulative skills
- To provide opportunities for children to gain control over their bodies
- To develop spatial awareness
- To develop hand/eye coordination

INTELLECTUAL DEVELOPMENT
- To develop concentration and listening skills
- To encourage creativity and use of imagination
- To develop observational skills
- To enable children to grasp mathematical and scientific concepts
- To develop language and reasoning skills
- To encourage learning through direct experience

developed their educational 'methods' and curriculum for just such children. Both these educationalists devised different but formally structured closed methods of education. In their pure form they have survived only in the private sector – at least in the UK, but like Froebel they both have training systems bearing their name.

Montessori saw children as existing in a separate miniature world and did not advocate group interaction until the child arrived at the notion independently – nor did she advocate much adult contribution – not even from the 'directresses' whom she trained in her systems and who set up the all-important environment in which the children were to develop.

The manager employed in either a Montessori or a Rudolf Steiner school will already have a method and a curriculum structure to guide their planning. The manager's involvement will therefore be as a guide and advisor ensuring that the presentation of the work is in sympathy with the needs of modern parents and children. Montessori herself would have been most reluctant to modify her approach, whatever the 1989 Act demanded in respect to parents. Steiner on the other hand believed that parents were natural educators and would have experienced no conflict.

Managers in charge of private day-care settings may have the most powerful voice in respect of the curriculum and elect for the 'eclectic' approach – incorporating the simplicity of the Montessori environment and equipment with the community spirit of Steiner, the flexibility of Froebel, and the active planning, doing and reviewing of Highscope.

The choices made will be very dependent on the ages of the children and the level of their development. All the pioneers agree that the child's development is precious in its own right – Froebel orders us that 'at every stage be that stage'. The child's development should not be accelerated but should be enjoyed with the child for its value in the totality of their life experiences.

Whichever early years theorist is favoured, the curriculum's aims will still adhere to the *ten common principles*, which are:

1. Childhood is a valid point of life and not merely a preparation for adulthood.
2. The whole child is important – physical, intellectual, emotional, social and spiritual.
3. Learning is not compartmentalised – everything is connected.
4. Intrinsic motivation resulting in self-directed activity is valued.
5. Self-discipline is emphasised.
6. There are specially receptive stages of development when periods of learning occur.
7. What the child can – as opposed to cannot – do is the starting point in their education.
8. All children have an inner life which emerges under favourable conditions.
9. The people, both adults and children, with whom the child interacts are of central importance.
10. The child's education is seen as an interaction between the child and the environment, including in particular other people and knowledge itself.

Tina Bruce in *Early Childhood Education* (Hodder and Stoughton, London, 1987) offers a most interesting resumé of the principles and an analysis of how each is supported by the work of all three pioneers.

As has constantly been noted throughout the text there is a great dearth of management research in the early years context. The opposite is true in respect of the curriculum. It is the manager's job to be aware of such research and development and to ensure, by whatever processes are at her disposal, that the children for whom she is responsible benefit from her awareness.

EVALUATION

Managers should constantly reassess the curriculum provision and planning in relation to children's needs and experiences. These, together with their records of children's development, will enable them to plan more effectively for the next stage of learning.

WHAT EXACTLY DO WE MEAN BY 'CURRICULUM'?

It is useful to be clear about what exactly is meant by the term 'curriculum'. In its broadest sense, curriculum is a total learning package constructed deliberately to enhance the development and facilitate the learning of an individual or a group of individuals.

For example, the curriculum of a module in a Child Care Course has three main components:

EXAMPLE OF A CURRICULUM OF A MODULE

1. Syllabus of the module	The list of the areas of knowledge the students will be taught.	■ Child Development, 0–8 years. ■ Social & Psychology factors affecting this development. ■ Educational philosophy of Frobel, Steiner and Montessori. ■ Reading list to reflect above.
2. Structure of the module	The shape or pattern of attendance.	■ Day Release ■ Short Full-Time ■ Evening Course ■ Distance Learning
3. Methodology for the module	How the learning is going to be delivered using the activities of the teacher and of the students.	■ Lecturers/expositions ■ Seminar Groups/Discussion Groups ■ Workshops/Films/Group Tasks ■ Group Activities/Tutorials/Projects ■ Visits & Exhibition of work

(Note: Methodology is not only what teachers do, but also what students do.)

There is also a value base. In child care there would be a strong ethical value base. In other vocational areas the value base may more appropriately be commercial.

All of the above – the syllabus, the physical attendance, the methods used and the 'own-time' activities such as reading, homework and other preparation – will be documented and will collectively form the *curriculum*.

HIDDEN CURRICULUM

In addition there is always a 'hidden curriculum', i.e. one that is not deliberately constructed or planned and is not written down but which happens anyway. In the example above the hidden curriculum might be making new friends, learning how groups work and learning how you function in a new group situation.

APPLICATION TO THE NURSERY

When applying this model to the early years it will be obvious that the methodology, i.e. the children's and adults' activities, will be by far the largest part of the whole curriculum.

Activity
Think of a course you have attended recently and consider which area of the curriculum contributed most to you as a whole person.
Was it:
■ the knowledge you gained
■ the activities you undertook
■ the group discussion or activities
or was it:
■ the chats over coffee
■ the new friends you made
■ the laughs you had?
Was this part of the set curriculum or the hidden curriculum?

We all learn most when we are enjoying the activity we are engaged in.

Play is the activity the children enjoy most and from which they learn most. They learn from:
■ all the activities and experiences they devise themselves
■ all the materials and resources provided by adults
■ all they see and hear around them
■ the language they use with their peers
■ the language adults use with them.

Play – as we have all been taught – is a child's work; it is extremely serious, totally absorbing and very necessary. It allows opportunities for children to:
■ form their first peer group
■ make discoveries about themselves and the world in which they live, in their own time and at their own pace

- organise and re-organise and support their experiences
- consolidate their learning
- collect and express their thoughts
- develop language and communication systems
- develop concentration and perseverance
- develop physical, social, emotional and intellectual skills through first-hand experiences.

The expertise needed in planning an early years curriculum is to manage the child's 'play' activities in such a way that they will lead to all of the above and will lay a sound foundation for future more structured learning. This will contribute to a confident young person progressing to a school environment.

The syllabus part of the curriculum for the under-5s will not differ much from that of older children. Only the methods and activities will vary with the children's age – the discipline areas are exactly the same.

So even for very young children the curriculum will have a syllabus that includes the examples on pages 80–82 (this list is not intended to be fully comprehensive).

If all the materials mentioned in delivering the pre-school methodology were assembled and laid out safely, they would produce the ideal environment for delivering the curriculum.

Activity
Make a list of all the equipment you might put together to provide one aspect of the early years' curriculum, e.g. Science.

It is the manager's responsibility to ensure that this rich environment to foster the child's development, is in place in the nursery. Remember that in providing a syllabus for very young children, attention must be paid to all aspects of the child, i.e.

PHYSICAL DEVELOPMENT
INTELLECTUAL DEVELOPMENT
EMOTIONAL DEVELOPMENT
SOCIAL DEVELOPMENT

As we have noted, it is impossible to separate one aspect of a child's development from another but the old much favoured mnemonic provides a model to structure reflection during the planning process.

GOOD PRACTICE

Special reference must be made to language. Language acquisition underpins all aspects of any early years' programme. Supported children will spontaneously provide a constant commentary to their activities. Much of a professional worker's skill is in extending this spontaneous talk, facilitating good language development. *Every adult is a teacher of language – a sombre thought.*

EXAMPLE OF A SYLLABUS FOR UNDER-5s

	Syllabus	Methodology
Some examples of Science:	■ how things float and sink ■ how things grow – plants and animals ■ how shadows form ■ how gravity works ■ how rainbows are made ■ how machines and computers work ■ how our bodies work	■ water – items with different properties ■ sand – wet and dry – different containers ■ plants – to grow outside and inside, in and out of soil ■ animals – to observe and care for ■ things going up – balloons and kites ■ things coming down – like rain and balls ■ computers and special programmes to work with ■ things to cook and bake with
Some examples of Mathematics:	■ how to count and rank things ■ how shapes and sizes work together – above, below, behind ■ how to calculate things	■ things to count and sort ■ shapes to name and label and make pictures with ■ things to rank and place in space ■ weighing and measuring things

continued

	Syllabus	Methodology
Some examples of Language:	■ how words carry meaning ■ how words in books carry stories and poems ■ how to talk ■ how not all people speak the same language	■ books to read and stories to tell ■ words to carry meanings on cards and on pages ■ words to symbolise real things ■ stories and rhymes to sing and chant ■ more than one language – written down, spoken and on tape
Some examples of Physical Development:	■ how to run and move about ■ how our bodies work and do things for us ■ what the parts of the body are called ■ how to move to music ■ how to climb and swing	■ music and movement ■ ball games ■ ring games ■ balancing games ■ outdoor activities ■ moving the body ■ running and skipping ■ taking turns on equipment
Some examples of Social Studies:	■ how you behave with other people ■ how other people behave with you, inside and outside, at the shops, at the theatre, at the library, on the bus ■ how people like to be respected ■ how people are different from each other ■ how people are similar ■ the 'social contract'	■ home corner to work in, shop to sell in ■ imaginative play and role play ■ codes of behaviour and rules in the nursery ■ outings to library, park, theatre, on a bus ■ play house

continued

Syllabus	Methodology
Some examples of The Arts:	
■ what colours are called and how they change when mixed ■ how to express things on paper ■ how to paint ■ how to act ■ how to make things ■ how to sing and make musical sounds	■ plays to perform ■ things to make ■ dough and Clay ■ painting with different paints ■ drawing different things ■ cutting and sticking ■ models to make

Management strategies for planning the curriculum

As with policies and procedures, it is very important that all the child care staff participate in developing and writing the curriculum. This should include students and volunteers (where appropriate).

This is important so that:

- everyone will have a sense of ownership of the curriculum and will deliver it with enthusiasm
- team work is fostered in this area, as in others, and no-one is excluded
- there is consistent approach to the work and also towards individual children
- curriculum planning becomes an integral part of staff development.
- the children benefit from all the available creativity of the staff.

The member of staff with the most appropriate background and skills should be given responsibility for organising the curriculum planning. This need not be the manager; in many ways results will be more controllable if someone else (a curriculum co-ordinator) undertakes this task. However, as the most experienced and senior member of staff, the manager should attend and contribute fully to all curriculum meetings to signal the high profile given to the children's learning within the centre. If the manager holds on to this work the planning process can so easily be deferred in the midst of the urgency of the hundred other daily tasks. When another professional holds curriculum as a special responsibility – with a reporting system – the work will happen without the manager needing to initiate it every time and the children will benefit accordingly. The reporting system is vital – it is important to delegate, not dump.

Delegating curriculum planning

This area is particularly appropriate for job enhancement. See also Chapter 3 on staff motivation.

TASKS OF THE CURRICULUM CO-ORDINATOR

It is this curriculum co-ordinator's job to convene the planning meetings. A *bare minimum* is one main planning meeting each term. At this meeting the term's work can be planned and a series of smaller meetings can be arranged for the work to progress.

GOOD PRACTICE

Even if the nursery is open for the whole year, the curriculum should still follow the traditional academic terms. It makes an excellent contrast for the children if a 'special' programme is written for the long academic break. This programme can be more orientated to small frequent outings and other seasonal activities.

There are three main reasons for the practice of keeping the academic terms for purposes of curriculum planning:
- to pace and structure the work
- to minimise disruption for children's holidays
- to prepare the children for school
- to facilitate progression.

The *annual planning cycle* has seven phases and will look something like this

1. September to October	Autumn Curriculum
2. October to December	Winter Curriculum
3. January to February	Winter Curriculum
4. February to March	Spring Curriculum
5. March to May	Spring Curriculum
6. May to July	Summer Curriculum
7. July to September	Special Programme

Activity
In a group examine the annual planning cycle and, thinking of the fun the children might have, suggest themes for each term or half-term. Be as frivolous as you like.

Care should be taken to avoid exact repetition year after year because:
- the long term staff will become stale
- new team members will not be making their full contribution to the work; they will feel excluded and their creativity will be wasted
- the resources will lack freshness
- the older children will become bored even if they do not consciously 'remember'.

However, a certain similarity from one year to the next is unavoidable, and even welcome, as children relate well to the familiar. Obviously, the religious festivals also recur and must be included each year.

CHOOSING A THEME FOR THE EARLY YEARS' CURRICULUM

A theme can be identified for each block, whether it be a whole or a half term. Themes can range from a major project to a small interest table.

A major project can involve all classes of a nursery or small groups, each working on a different related topic. It may involve all members of staff and cover all areas of the curriculum.

An isolated project may be relevant to a particular group, and not related to the general theme for the term.

A spontaneous interest table may focus on a topical issue which arises within the group.

GOOD PRACTICE

A calendar of religious festivals is now easily available and this is an invaluable resource in the planning process and as part of the multi-cultural display.

It is very good practice to be non-selective in recognition and celebration of religious festivals whichever culture predominates in the nursery. All our children are growing up in a multi-cultural society, and the earlier they develop mutual knowledge of each other, the earlier they will develop mutual trust and respect.

CASE STUDY

'As part of an inspection team I visited a quite prestigious nursery one early December. I found the staff energetically putting up Christmas decorations. I complimented the manager on how pretty they looked and on how hard the staff were working. I followed this by asking "Do you celebrate other festivals in the centre?". "Oh yes, Easter" she replied.'

Before the main planning meeting the curriculum co-ordinator should notify staff and

■ prepare in advance a structure for the work, e.g. six or twelve week programmes, half term, or one term. Half terms allow flexibility and ease of movement of progressing children (and possibly also staff)

■ ask that they give some thought to the task and bring curriculum ideas with them because everyone will benefit from time spent thinking through aims and objectives

■ give the start and finish times of the meeting and adhere to these.

Resources for use at the planning meeting
1. A copy of the National Curriculum, to stimulate ideas and act as a reminder of the children's future expectations.
2. A copy of 'Desirable Outcomes for Childrens Learning' (SCAA document, 1995), to stimulate ideas, act as a reminder, provide parameters and set standards.

3. Other resource books and professional journals, to stimulate ideas and confirm standards, e.g. *Nursery World*.
4. Large sheets of paper/flip charts, and a selection of writing equipment.
5. Other resource materials, e.g. religious festivals calendar, details of planned events in the community, local library, children's theatres, exhibitions on offer etc.

At the end of the meeting there should be:
1. A theme selected which must be attractive to the adult, and potentially attractive to the children. It must be offered at a suitable intellectual level for the age of the group. Themes could be:
   - seasonal
   - topical, e.g. something that will be covered in the media
   - linked to a particular child, or relevant to the group at that time
   - linked to some object or collection or hobby
   - related to a specific area of the curriculum
   - based specifically on one or more of the senses
   - designed to provide imaginative play stimulus
   - designed to encourage self awareness or awareness of others
   - selected to introduce an aspect of the child's wider environment and community.
2. A firm commitment from colleagues to contribute themselves and the resources to the work.
3. A programme of smaller meetings to work out details of visits and outings and so forth.
4. A date when the final programme will appear. The curriculum co-ordinator can now:
   - start collecting resources
   - involve children in the planning and preparation
   - involve parents
   - plan to involve the wider environment and community, e.g. by visits out and bringing visitors in
   - plan for 'hands-on' and imaginative play experiences for the children
   - be prepared to be flexible as the planning proceeds.

WHY DO WE USE PROJECTS AND THEMES?

- With well thought out objectives, children will grow in physical, intellectual, emotional and social development.
- Opportunities exist to extend language, general knowledge and understanding, through familiar topics, and to introduce the wider environment and community.
- With thoughtful planning all, or most, areas of the curriculum can be incorporated.
- Children can be encouraged to develop sensory awareness using all five senses.
- Children can be involved at all stages; then they acquire new concepts, and are curious to find out more.

- The eye-catching displays produced will attract children and parents, and will hold their interest.
- Parents can be invited and encouraged to be involved.
- Particular themes can be of value or special interest to individual children giving them affirmation.
- A theme provides a focus and encourages co-operation from the whole team.
- Themes are fun, with opportunities in all categories of play, and for all levels of players.

In the nursery

One method of writing-up the plan is to produce a spider diagram. Sample 36 illustrates a seven week programme using Transport as the theme, chosen because of the interest of one group of children in the nursery concerned.

See Sample 36, page 198.

Activity

With a partner, chose a topic using the system above and brainstorm a programme for a group of children of a specified age. If you are ambitious, you could go on to design the curriculum for the school.

GOOD PRACTICE

Where it is at all possible, the work of planning the curriculum should be done in nursery time. Where this is not possible, some recognition should be made of the staff's attendance out of hours.
Either:
a) it should be made clear on the appointment of staff that some evening attendance is expected, e.g. for parents' evenings, planning meetings and social events
b) time off in lieu may be given to staff at a time convenient to the nursery, if finances allow
c) if it is more appropriate and possible, overtime can be paid.
This is a difficult and sensitive issue. Whatever management policy is adopted, time for planning meetings must be made. The curriculum should never be imposed on the staff. Where job descriptions and circumstances permit, option (a) above is by far the best solution.

It is very poor practice and quite unacceptable to offer the children unplanned or inadequately planned work. Their development will undoubtedly suffer and learning opportunities will be lost forever. There will also be a great loss of morale among the staff and missed opportunities for team building.

The Schools Council Assessment Authority (SCAA) and implications for the manager's role

In Autumn 1995 the Schools Council Assessment Authority (SCAA) produced a discussion document offering guidance to providers of *Desirable Outcomes for Children's Learning* to be achieved by the time they entered school. The SCAA claims that what they are offering is not strictly a curriculum, as that is the role of the provider, but they suggest educational activities likely to lead to the 'desirable outcome'.

The document also emphasises the importance of partnership with parents and suggests the following ten significant features of good practice.

1. Adults working in the setting and parents have a statement which outlines the aims, objectives and content of the curriculum, how it is taught and how children's progress and achievement are assessed, recorded and shared with parents and the schools to which the children will progress.

In the nursery
Examples of recording systems which can be adapted to meet your own needs are provided in Appendix A.
   See Samples 34, 37–39 and 41, pages 196, 199–209 and 211.

2. Parents' fundamental role in their children's education is acknowledged and a partnership, based on shared understanding, mutual respect and dialogue, is developed.

In the nursery
This partnership is also required under the Children Act and formalised in policy statements.
   See Sample 4, page 155.

3. Children feel secure, valued and confident and develop a sense of achievement through learning which is a pleasurable and rewarding experience both within the nursery setting and at home.

4. There is good liaison with other agencies and carers, such as health visitors and childminders, and these contacts are used in planning opportunities for learning for individual children.

5. Children participate in a range of activities which take due account of their developing physical, intellectual, emotional and social abilities (PIES).

6. Children are encouraged to think and talk about their learning and to develop self control and independence. They are given appropriate periods of time for learning through sustained involvement in concentrated activity. Approaches to teaching include recognition of the value of providing first-hand experiences, of giving direction and using play and talk as media for learning.

7. Children's progress is assessed and recorded through frequent observation and is shared regularly with parents.
8. Early identification of children's particular needs leads to appropriate intervention and support.

9. Successful links with the next stage of education are maintained.
10. The physical environment supports learning with appropriate space, facilities and equipment and is organised with due regard to health and safety.

These ten significant features will be found in all quality child care centres. They will be recognised during 'light touch' inspections and will attract government funding in whatever setting they are provided.

The curriculum areas the SCAA identifies are very similar to the areas already discussed, but are written in terms of positive outcomes, i.e. actual abilities the children should have by the end of their nursery experience.

Activity
Using a curriculum plan or programme with which you are familiar, translate it into terms of positive outcomes using the identified outcomes on pages 90–95 as a model.

The desirable outcomes for children's learning on entering compulsory schooling fall into six areas:

SCAA Curriculum	Traditional Curriculum
Personal and Social Development	Social Studies
Language and Literacy	Language
Mathematics	Mathematics
Knowledge and Understanding of the World	All Sciences, Geography, History
Physical Development	Physical Development
Creativity	The Arts

Activity
Compare the SCAA curriculum (pages 90–95) with the traditional curriculum (pages 80–82) and note the difference in emphasis which occurs when the 'learning outcomes' are paramount, i.e not what the teacher has taught but what the child can do.

PERSONAL AND SOCIAL DEVELOPMENT

These outcomes focus on children learning how to work, play and co-operate with others. They cover important aspects of personal and social development including the development of personal values, and an understanding of self and others.

'Children are confident and able to establish effective relationships with other children and with adults. They work as part of a group and independently, are able to concentrate for sustained periods, to explore new learning and to seek help where needed. They are independent in dressing themselves and in matters of personal hygiene.

Children respect others, take turns, share fairly and behave appropriately, developing a sense of what is right and what is wrong, and why. They treat living things and property with care and concern. They take part, where appropriate, in cultural and religious events and sometimes show feelings, such as wonder, pleasure and sorrow.'

Personal and Social Development Outcomes can be achieved by
- creating situations for the children to be independent, e.g. toilet training
- providing opportunities to discuss the past, both immediate and earlier
- providing opportunities to discuss the future, both immediate and later
- providing opportunities to handle artefacts from different ages and cultures
- creating situations to observe place in the community and the wider world
- creating situations where the children can improve the natural environment
- encouraging children to question decisions
- encouraging children to appreciate what is fair and equitable
- creating situations for co-operative and collaborative play
- providing opportunities for children to express themselves through different mediums, e.g. art, music, imaginative play
- providing opportunities for children to learn to control their emotions
- providing opportunities for children to understand the wider world and issues within it
- providing role play opportunities
- creating situations where the children can value other people
- providing opportunities for children to have a positive self-image and worth.

LANGUAGE AND LITERACY

These fundamentally important outcomes focus on children's developing competence in talking and listening and in becoming readers and writers. Many of the other outcomes also make a vital contribution to the successful development of literacy.

'In small and large groups, children listen attentively and talk about their experiences. They use a growing vocabulary with increasing fluency to express thoughts and convey meaning to the listener. They listen and respond, with enjoyment, to stories, songs, nursery rhymes and poems. They make up their own stories and take part in role play with confidence.

Children enjoy books and understand that words and pictures carry meaning. They handle books carefully and know that in English, print is read from left to right hand, top to bottom. They begin to associate sounds with patterns in rhymes, with syllables, and with words and letters. They recognise their own names and some familiar words. They recognise letters of the alphabet by shape and sound. In their writing they use pictures, symbols, familiar words and letters, to communicate meaning. They write their names with appropriate use of upper and lower case letters.'

Language and Literacy Learning Outcomes can be achieved by
- making the whole environment a place where language and literacy are prominent and useful
- valuing the accent and mother tongue of each child and giving priority to their first language
- encouraging talk across the curriculum
- providing a positive role model for the correct use of language
- creating situations and providing equipment that encourage talk in imaginative contexts
- providing conversation partners, both adults and peers
- encouraging talk for different proposes, e.g. to recall, predict, describe, imagine and project
- encouraging children to listen to others
- introducing a variety of language structures including story, rhyme, non-fiction and poetry
- introducing and discussing media, e.g. radio and cassettes
- creating an environment where books and reading are enjoyed and valued
- sharing books with children on a regular basis, encouraging children to participate and answering their questions
- giving children a wide experience of many types of books and opportunities to browse and talk about books
- giving children the space and time to use books alone
- involving parents in developing their children's Emergent Reading Skills (ERS)
- encouraging the children to participate in writing activities
- acting as scribes so that children's own ideas can be written down and read by others
- encouraging children to explore and experiment with mark-making
- providing situations where writing is useful and relevant
- introducing children to the word processor
- having an adult available to provide a model of writing behaviour.

MATHEMATICS

These outcomes cover important aspects of mathematical understanding and provide the foundation for numeracy. They focus on achievement through practical activities and on using and understanding language in the development of simple mathematical ideas.

'Children use simple mathematical language, such as circle, in front of, bigger than and more, to describe shape, position, size and quantity. They recognise and recreate patterns. They are familiar with rhymes, songs, stories, counting games and activities. They compare, sort, match, order, sequence and count using everyday objects. They recognise and use numbers to 10 and are familiar with large numbers from their everyday lives, for example, their birthdays and house numbers. Through practical activities children understand and record numbers, begin to show awareness of number operations, such as addition and subtraction, and begin to use the language involved.'

Mathematical Learning Outcomes can be achieved by

■ devising meaningful contexts where maths is relevant
■ planning an environment where maths is useful in all areas
■ encouraging children to participate in everyday maths; maths is all around us
■ encouraging strategies such as estimating and looking for patterns
■ encouraging perceptual judgements and logical reasoning
■ introducing number names by singing rhymes and sharing stories
■ encouraging counting forward and counting back using rhymes and games
■ encouraging children to record the number of objects, and being aware of the arbitrary systems they may devise to do this
■ giving children the opportunity to compare objects for size, weight etc.
■ introducing the function of measures by involving children in situations that demand their use, e.g. baking, shopping, making models
■ providing imaginative and role-play contexts where the use of measures is needed
■ encouraging children to look for patterns in the environment
■ creating situations where patterns serve a purpose
■ providing opportunities to explore shapes and three-dimensional concepts
■ offering materials for building and changing shapes
■ providing opportunities to discover spatial relationships including above, below, distance and location
■ providing opportunities for children to record their mathematical activities and experiences in different ways, e.g. talk, recording with real objects, representing in paint or clay.

KNOWLEDGE AND UNDERSTANDING OF THE WORLD

These outcomes relate to children's developing knowledge and understanding of their environment, other people and features of the natural and made world. They include the development of skills for later learning in history, geography, science and technology.

'Children talk about where they live, their environment, their families and past and present events in their own lives. They explore and recognise features of the natural and made world and observe similarities, differences, patterns and change. They talk about their observations, sometimes recording them, and ask questions about why things happen and how things work. They use skills, such as cutting, joining, folding and building, and use a range of appropriate tools safely. They use tape recorders, computers and other technology, where appropriate.

Knowledge and Understanding of the World Learning Outcomes can be achieved by

- creating situations where tools, equipment and materials can be used safely
- providing a wide variety of construction toys
- creating situations where children are shown how to use materials for different purposes
- encouraging children to recognise that materials have different properties, e.g. colour, texture, flexibility
- creating situations where children begin to work co-operatively together
- encouraging children to develop information technology skills
- encouraging children to be interested in technology irrespective of gender, cultural, intellectual or social differences
- creating situations where children have opportunity to express their ideas about what they might do to meet an identified need or opportunity
- encouraging children to communicate through descriptive language what they like/dislike about their environment
- encouraging children to explore familiar situations
- encouraging children to observe, wonder, speculate and ask
- encouraging children to explore the world around them to create knowledge out of their own questions, thoughts and experiences
- introducing basic physical processes, e.g magnetism, light, sound, forces and their effects
- giving children time and space to make discoveries
- making children aware of the environment and issues related to it, e.g. recycling
- creating situations and providing equipment that encourages scientific talk and play
- providing opportunities to discuss health issues and our bodies, e.g. diet, visits from dentist etc.
- providing opportunities to grow plants from cuttings, seeds, bulbs etc. and in a variety of mediums, e.g. compost, sand, water and differing habitats
- providing opportunities to care for living creatures
- providing opportunities to observe and discuss life cycles of different species
- providing opportunities to discuss their growth and development
- providing experiences of devices which move and experiences of the natural force of gravity
- providing scientific books for information
- telling stories or rhymes about plants and animals
- questioning and talking about experiences with materials, animals and plants
- providing tape recordings for information.

PHYSICAL DEVELOPMENT

These outcomes relate to children's developing physical control, mobility, awareness of space and manipulative skills in indoor and outdoor environments.

'Children move confidently and imaginatively with increasing control and co-ordination and an awareness of space and others. They use a range of small and large equipment, such as wheeled toys, beanbags, balls and balancing and climbing apparatus, with increasing skill. They handle small tools and objects, such as pencils, paintbrushes and scissors, with increasing control.'	*Physical Development Learning Outcomes* can be achieved by ■ providing opportunities for gross motor skills development ■ providing opportunities for fine manipulative skills development ■ awareness of opportunities during the day-to-day routine of dressing/undressing ■ encouraging play indoors/outdoors to improve hand-eye co-ordination ■ encouraging children to use their bodies fully, to increase stamina ■ encouraging children to understand that good hygiene leads to care of their bodies ■ encouraging children to move in new and different ways ■ providing information, e.g. songs and rhymes, and experiences to increase physical awareness ■ helping children to increase their emotional self-awareness and to cope with this, e.g. success, failure, determination etc. ■ encouraging confidence in skills of locomotion and balance, in pace with developing skills.

CREATIVITY

These outcomes relate to the development of children's imagination and their ability to express ideas and feelings in creative ways. Many are also closely linked to literacy and children's physical development.

'Children use a range of materials, suitable tools and resources to represent what they see, hear, touch and feel. They explore colour, texture, shape, form and space in two and three dimensions. They respond to rhythm in music and dance and use imagination in stories and role play.'

Creativity Outcomes can be achieved by

- stimulating the children's imagination by making the environment stimulating and enriching
- creating opportunities for children to work in two and three dimensions
- appreciating and valuing children's work as their individual response, and assisting parents to do likewise
- providing opportunities for children to work practically and imaginatively with a wide range of materials and tools
- encouraging expression of ideas, thoughts and feelings
- providing opportunities for children to record images and ideas from the world around them
- providing opportunities to experience different musical instruments and the sounds they make and to make their own sound-making apparatus
- providing opportunities for quiet times to listen and respond appropriately to music and other experiences
- creating attractive displays of children's work
- use of media where appropriate.

THE ABLE CHILD

For children able to go beyond the 'desirable outcome', the SCAA suggest it is appropriate to provide the opportunities already planned and published for Key Stage 1 programmes of study in the National Curriculum.

PARENTAL INVOLVEMENT IN THE CURRICULUM

There are many ways to involve parents, seek their advice and elicit their opinion on the curriculum and their own child's particular needs.

Open evenings

It is good practice to explain the curriculum to parents. Do not hesitate to use the names of academic subjects as parents often do not always perceive early maths, science or literacy in the children's work and play.

Display

The curriculum plan should be on show in the nursery and each work area should be labelled with some explanation at adult height.

Personal involvement

Many parents will be happy to come into the nursery and contribute from their own expertise and culture.

CASE STUDY

'A particularly talented nursery professional I know had a vicar's child in her nursery and on occasions when the nursery celebrated a 'wedding' this parent would attend appropriately dressed and 'officiate' at the ceremony.

This was a truly wonderful experience for the children. They had science with the cake making, maths in the table laying and guest counting, language in the stories and rhymes on the subject, creativity in the music, in the invitations and decorations, all the personal and social development anyone could ask for in the dressing up and role playing involved from uncles to brides and grannies. They also had the vicar's delighted interest and affirmation of their work.

This same teacher invited parents to cook foods from different countries and teach children in small groups in the process. This was during a term when the theme was Foods.'

Children's work

The children's work should be sent home in protective cases and discussed with the parents. Their work should be mounted and displayed on the walls. Written explanation should be attached where needed, particularly verbatim quotations from the children themselves.

Children's records
Open records are most suitable for the children's records. These should be completed by their key-worker and parents kept informed of their work.

Shared homework
There are several ways to involve the parents in work with the children at home. Many of these methods have been developed for infant school children but adapt readily for the younger child.

A good example of this is IMPACT MATHS:

Interactive
Maths for
Parents
And
Children and
Teachers

This system is one in which the child takes home enough information to 'teach' the parent some aspect of maths from that day's work. The parent and child undertake the exercise together and complete the written part of the work; this is then returned to school for the teacher to mark. Similar schemes can be devised for other subjects depending on the local conditions.

In the nursery

Reading together for homework is always a good idea. Parents can be asked to complete a feedback sheet. Nursery books on the selected theme can be 'borrowed' to take home (in plastic envelopes) and returned after reading, e.g. over a week-end.

See Sample 40, page 210.

KEYS TO GOOD PRACTICE

■ Curriculum planning must take place and must be given a high profile in the centre.
■ The curriculum should be published in the nursery on the display board.
■ All child care staff should be involved in the curriculum, including students.
■ All parents should be involved, particularly if they can contribute something special for all the children.
■ All children should be involved. Mutual respect between parent and child can be fostered if together they contribute to the nursery's work.
■ Staff should be recognised for their contribution. A curriculum co-ordinator should be identified and, if appropriate, given special training for this important role.
■ Children's development should be assessed at intervals agreed with the parents.

- Records should be given to parents and made available to destination schools.
- Care should be taken that the nursery satisfies the SCAA requirements.

7 RECRUITING STAFF FOR QUALITY CHILD CARE

What this chapter covers:
- **initiating the selection process**
- **interviewing and choosing staff**
- **induction and mentoring of new staff**
- **teams, team roles and team building**

This chapter is about what is, in any manager's opinion, the most important task they ever perform – the one to be undertaken with the greatest care, with the clearest head and with the most intelligence. This is the task of choosing the staff, settling them in, supporting their work and making them into real team members.

It is rare, but not unknown, to be in a position to choose all staff from scratch. It is more likely that new members will be joining an existing team, and for this reason some suggestions about team roles are included. Fortunately, their existing inter-personal expertise makes this work much less daunting for new child care managers than for many others.

Initiating the selection process

Selection is often thought of in its narrowest context, i.e. of using techniques which enable the selector to choose one candidate rather than another for a particular post. This view is restrictive as it places emphasis on the needs of the selectors at the expense of those of the candidates, who also require information on which they can base their decision as to whether they wish to accept the post being offered.

To satisfy both these aspects, selection needs to be viewed as a two-way process which involves both the giving and receiving of information, so that the post is filled by the applicant who:
- is most capable of satisfying the requirements of the post (preferably in both the short and long term)
- will fit into the environment and will perform well with existing colleagues
- wishes to accept the post based on knowledge and impressions gained and their own assessment of how they will fit into the organisation and contribute to its objectives.

By it's very nature, the child care profession is labour intensive. There can be little argument concerning the importance of the contribution which staff make to the centre's level of performance. The standards accepted by staff become the standards of the institution and these directly affect the satisfaction of parents.

In addition, the future quality of the service and life of the children will be governed directly by the ability of staff to cope with the demands of any future changes and to provide quality role models for the children. For this reason the selection of staff is one of the most important decisions made by those in management positions within nurseries.

Unfortunately, those making appointments are often so busy that they have little time for reflection and make their decisions intuitively on small samples of behaviour, which are haphazard and in no way serve as indicators of future performance.

To reduce the risks involved in selection there is a need for a system which supports those having to make decisions by presenting them with the best information possible.

However, before we explore selection systems, it is worthwhile pointing out that there is no such thing as an 'off-the-peg' system which can be applied to all situations. The 'closest fit' (between system and situation) can only be achieved by matching it against the particular needs of the nursery: it's rules, mode of operation, the kind of post under consideration, the particular skills needed and the role the person will occupy in the team.

A further factor worth stressing is that some nurseries will be subject to union or local authority agreements which lay down steps to be followed in promoting or replacing staff. Although there are fewer and fewer in this category, these agreements will influence the systems used and should be checked before the work begins.

Where choice is available, it is worthwhile first considering the advantages and disadvantages of selecting internal or external candidates, as shown below.

Internal candidates

Advantages
Shows that promotion is possible
Gives individual staff members an incentive
You know what you are getting
The applicant knows what to expect
Sends a good signal to future external candidates

Disadvantages
May limit choice
May make the organisation inward-looking
There is no injection of new blood
May result in staff with positions 'locked up'

External candidates

Advantages
New skills and experience are brought into the organisation
Helps to remind others that they have not proved themselves sufficiently

Disadvantages
It is difficult for one person to have much impact on an existing organisation
Reminds people that the organisation and its service are more important than they are
Selection process may result in a candidate who is no better than those already in the organisation
May cause dissatisfaction and a view that effort will not be rewarded

THE PROCESS OF SELECTION

Bearing in mind the constraints already discussed, the process of selection would include the activities shown in the following flow diagram.

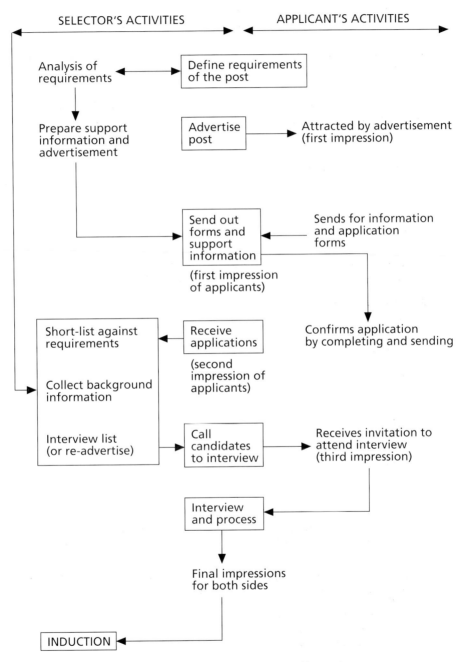

Flow diagram showing the selection process for staff members

If the nursery is small (fewer than twelve staff) everyone should be consulted in an open manner.

DEFINING THE REQUIREMENTS OF THE POST

The starting point for selection must be some form of study of the post to be filled. However, do not be overcome by the techniques available; allow common sense to prevail.

BACK-UP INFORMATION

The advertisement

The advertisement should be based on the requirements of the job specification and should be designed and worded in such a way that it will appeal to the kind of people you are hoping to attract. At a minimum it should include:

- the title of the post
- an indication of the type of work
- the starting date
- the name of the establishment or department
- the grade and salary
- where and how to obtain further information
- the closing date for applications.

Support information on the post

This will be based on the job requirements and should include information on the conditions under which the duties are to be carried out. This will generally comprise:

- specific detailed requirements of the post in the short and long term, e.g. present duties, future development
- general duties associated with the post, e.g. responsibilities for curriculum, equipment or stock control
- where the post fits into the organisation and where it may lead to in the future.

Support material

This material should be aimed at providing background information on the authority and the nursery in which the post is located. The kind of information given should generally include:

- description of geographical location
- catchment area and population
- number of nursery and support staff
- description of range of work
- resources
- buildings and accommodation

- transport facilities
- organisational features, if appropriate
- governors (if applicable) or accounting systems
- internal organisation, if appropriate
- conditions of service
- relocation expenses, if appropriate.

ADVERTISING THE POST

To attract the right people, the advertisement must be placed in the most appropriate journal or newspaper at the right time. This means that the target audience should be identified as closely as possible before placing the advertisement.

Remember that there are recruiting seasons for some candidates, such as graduates or students direct from training establishments.

SENDING OUT FORMS AND INFORMATION

A policy decision should be taken before placing the advertisement as to whether enquiries for forms should be accompanied by a stamped-addressed envelope and whether telephone requests for forms will be accepted.

GOOD PRACTICE

Whichever of the above options is chosen, a careful record should be kept of the number of enquiries for information and forms and of the names and addresses. These may be useful later should the post be re-advertised. The number of enquiries can be matched against the number of actual applications. These records will also give valuable information as to which advertising vehicle gives the best results for the nursery.

SHORT-LISTING CANDIDATES FROM THE RECEIVED FORMS

Depending on the size of the response, considerable time can be saved if a system has been devised for sifting the information contained in the incoming applications.

Various ranking systems can be used, based on cross-referencing the information and matching it against the requirements of the post. However, care must be taken as all of the information about the candidates is not available at this stage and the process is reduced to considering the following:
- personal details
- education/training
- qualifications
- experience to date
- presentation of information.

If the number of candidates is large and finance is available, preliminary interviews may also be used to prepare the final short-list of candidates.

COLLECTING BACKGROUND INFORMATION

People vary in the way they check references, with some doing so before the interview and others afterwards.

There are arguments for and against both methods. One thing is clear: considerable tact may be needed, as reference checking can have an adverse effect on the careers of external candidates whose employers do not know that they are job hunting.

A further point is that in these days of open references, research may be necessary to assess their real value.

CALLING CANDIDATES FOR INTERVIEW

It is worth giving careful thought to the method of calling candidates for interview, as this helps you establish the image of the nursery.

The invitation should include information on the timetable and method of interviewing. It may also include the number of others on the short-list and should include a map of the location, travelling arrangements and where to obtain accommodation, if this is necessary.

PRESENTATION OF INFORMATION ON THE UNIT/ORGANISATION

This is the most important stage from the point of view of the candidates, as it is their opportunity to collect information about the unit and its working environment.

It is the period in which they assess whether the information given to them before their arrival represents a true picture of the post and the circumstances under which the duties will be carried out.

The programme of presentation will vary depending upon the number of candidates, the level of the post and the resources available for interviewing.

GOOD PRACTICE

A welcoming programme for the candidates should be arranged. This could include:

- coffee on arrival at centre
- welcome by manager or head of department and general description of the centre and its work
- tour of the centre with particular emphasis on those parts directly affecting the post on offer
- meeting with future colleagues
- informal discussions
- formal interviews.

In this important area many employers also ask candidates to attend the nursery for one or two sessions so that their performance can be observed and their interaction with the children checked.

Interviewing and choosing staff

ESSENTIALS OF GOOD INTERVIEWING

- Every interview has a purpose. Make sure you know what you want from your interview and frame your questions accordingly.
- Be prepared. Find out what you can about candidates from their records and make a note of the main questions you wish to put to them.
- Ensure that you are not going to be interrupted and that the interview room is free of distractions.
- Arrange the seating so that you and the candidate can see and hear each other clearly.
- Try to establish a good rapport with the candidate and maintain it throughout. An interview is not an interrogation, nor is it an excuse for playing power games.
- Ask questions that allow candidates to give full answers. Avoid asking too many questions that require only a one-word reply. Also avoid multiple, trick and leading questions that force candidates to answer in the way you want (see 'open' and 'closed' questions later in this chapter).
- Let candidates do most of the talking and show by voice, facial expression and gesture that you are listening to what they are telling you.

GOOD PRACTICE

Ensure that you have developed your skills in this area prior to embarking on an interview programme. The activity below will give you some practice.

- Should a candidate become upset or hostile, remain calm, objective and detached.
- Avoid any references to the candidate's appearance, sex, age, religion or race.
- End the interview in the same friendly manner in which it began and, no matter what the nature of the interview, always leave the candidates with their dignity and self-esteem intact.

GOOD PRACTICE

Discussion concerning the child care needs of the candidate can take place *after* the appointment has been made. If concessionary places are available, information about this arrangement should be set out in the Terms and Conditions of Service.

Activity
This activity is designed to develop your active listening skills.
Interviewing and listening skills are essential for a good manager. The next time you are conducting an interview (or appraisal interview – see Chapter 8)

follow these guidelines.

- Have sufficient empathy to create surroundings which are comfortable an appropriate to the kind of interview you are conducting.
- Decide what you want to achieve from the interview in advance and plan it properly.
- Leave yourself time and freedom from interruptions so that you can concentrate on the interviewee's problems and not your own.
- Recognise and acknowledge any prejudices you may harbour and keep them out of the interview, to the best of your ability.
- Do not accept everything the interviewee tells you at face value. Probe for evasions, questions cliches and examine half-truths.
- Be patient. Do not interrupt. Let the interviewee finish before asking the next question.
- Be tolerant. You may not like what the interviewee is saying, or even the interviewee, but put your personal feelings aside.
- Finally, be comfortable with yourself. The more at ease you are with yourself, the more at ease interviewees will be with you and the more open their answers will be.

SELECTION AND OFFER

Having chosen their favoured candidate, most organisations go through the offer and acceptance stage before dismissing the other candidates. This is done so that a follow-up offer can be made immediately to the second candidate if the first refuses the post.

GOOD PRACTICE

It is courteous at this stage for the manager or senior member of staff to thank the unsuccessful candidates and wish them well in the future. Constructive feedback on interview performance should be offered.

Induction and mentoring of new staff

Obviously, your system does not end with the appointment. Steps should be taken to get the selected candidate eased into the requirements of the post and settled into the nursery. You will have (hopefully) appointed someone whose ethics, values and performance mesh with those of the organisation. Recognise that:

- the appointee now needs to be established and consolidated on a foundation of mutual respect and trust
- it takes time and communication to establish rapport
- this new relationship is crucial to the success of your team and it is worth investing time and effort in the early stages.

It is worth investing time and effort also into a good induction programme, as it will meet important objectives, such as gaining greater employee loyalty, developing a stronger managerial base for future promotions or ending gender and racial inequalities. Later on, you may be expecting your new recruit to participate in recruiting and developing their own replacement as they move up the career ladder, so it is important to establish solid foundations.

Induction generally falls into two parts. The period between the appointment and taking up the post should be used for providing information on timetables, curriculum matters and other general information. A visit to the centre is useful for giving this information if it can be arranged. For the initial period in post, junior members of staff may be placed under the general guidance of a colleague whom they can call on for help with minor problems. This is known as *mentoring*.

Large nurseries or day care centres may have formal induction programmes covering the first weeks in the post. Alternatively, you may have to invent a programme for your new member of staff and this is best done *together* with that new member of staff.

In the nursery

With any new team member, it is important – on day one – to outline the expectations and limits of both the individual concerned and the existing team. One good way is to write down what you expect of the new employee and, perhaps more importantly, what your new recruit can (and is prepared to) offer. Go gently on formalising the relationship; some people may balk at the idea of having too many demands put upon them in the early stages. In any case, this 'agreement' will, obviously, change and be superseded as the new staff member settles into the job. Ideally, your relationship is going to be a long term one. Use an appropriate job description for this purpose.
See Samples 42–47, pages 212–220.

GOOD PRACTICE

Try to put yourself into the new person's shoes and anticipate their needs. It is natural for the new recruit to suffer from a feeling of isolation at first in the new environment. This is where a mentor becomes invaluable.

A mentor is someone who can challenge, support, advise, motivate and encourage your new member of staff. It must be someone who understands the work and believes in the potential of the new recruit. A mentor will provide a safe harbour for the new team member – a space to ask questions, think out loud, make mistakes without feeling embarrassed or quashed. A good mentor will view the new recruit objectively and give constructive feedback along with general guidance.

In the nursery

The mentor could be you – the nursery manager – but it is generally more effective if it is a colleague who is more senior than the new recruit (but not intimidating) or who is at the same level but who has been in the job for long enough to know the ropes. If the mentor is also the manager of the recruit, the recruit will be so anxious to please that they may find it difficult to ask unguarded questions. Similarly, do not put a new recruit into the care of a mentor who is already a friend of the new recruit (for instance, knew them at college) as true friends are rarely objective enough about each other. Use Samples 58–60 (which can be adapted for your own purposes) as a system for mentoring the skills of the new staff member.

See Samples 58–60, pages 234–241.

Teams, team roles and team building

We commonly use the expression 'the whole is greater than the sum of the parts' without stopping to consider what it might mean. The importance of having an effective team in a child care context cannot be underestimated. Here we will explore management theory that will assist the manager in putting together a good whole – a good team.

The concept of 'team' can be quite elusive: it is evident that people may function as a team without being part of a working group. Conversely people may belong to the same working group without constituting a team. The essence of a team is that its members form a co-operative association through a division of labour that best reflects the contribution that each can make towards the common objective. The members do not need to be present at the same place and at the same time to enable the team to function.

THE CHARACTERISTICS OF A TEAM

It is helpful to explore the characteristics of a team. In any organisation a good team will:

- work together
- share a common aim
- co-operate with others
- share/communicate/support between it's members
- have motivation for the task in hand
- have catalytic relationships so that new ideas are extended
- be committed to the task and the team
- be comprised of members who each understand their own role in the team and are reliable in it
- complete the task.

Clearly if a team does not or will not fulfill these criteria then it will not be a good team and will not best serve the needs of the organisation. Management theorists have, therefore, spent time and effort working out how and why teams work.

TEAM ROLE MODELS

A theorist called Meredith Belbin spent many years observing teams at work and re-designing these teams to see if productivity improved. From this work he built a *team role model* (1981) which identifies how individuals are likely to work within a team and how to put together combinations of individuals to get the best results.

Most teams are commonly made up of members holding particular roles. They are there by virtue of the position or responsibilities they represent. No overall sense of design governs the composition of the group which, in human terms, is little more than a random collection of people with as wide a spread of human foibles and personality characteristics as one might expect to find in the population at large.

Nevertheless it is clear that the compatibility of members of the team is crucial to its effectiveness. The question of the interaction of members within a team becomes more important the more often a team meets. It is a subject of no less importance than whether members of a team are qualified to be Nursery Assistants or Officers-in-Charge. The problem is that human compatibility is more difficult to assess than technical competence. Belbin's experiments and fieldwork give some leads on how the subject of compatibility within teams might be approached.

Belbin's studies showed that there are eight 'team roles' that people will assume in a group, as listed below.

Resource Investigator (RI): the team member who explores and reports on ideas or developments outside the group; good at making external contacts and at conducting negotiations; usually outgoing and relaxed, with a strong inquisitive sense; always ready to see the possibilities inherent in anything new.

Co-ordinator (Co): the person who controls the way the team moves forwards towards it's objectives by making the best use of the team's resources; good at recognising where the team's strengths and weaknesses lie; good at ensuring that the best use is made of the potential of each member of the team; sometimes acts as the chairperson of the group but need not be the official leader of the team; this person talks easily, listens carefully and basically trusts people.

Shaper (SH): this person shapes the way in which the team effort is applied, directing attention to the setting of objectives and priorities and seeking to impose some shape or pattern on group discussion and on the outcome of group activities; anxious, dominant and extrovert, full of nervous energy, the shaper is outgoing, emotional, impulsive and impatient but has nervous energy and commitment which ensure that the team remains task-orientated and able to achieve.

Completer/finisher (CF): protects the team from mistakes of both commission and omission, actively searches for aspects of works which require a more than usual degree of attention and maintains a sense of urgency within the team; has a sense of concern with order and purpose and usually has good self-control and strength of character; a strong concern for detail and a tendency to check everything personally to make sure that nothing has been overlooked.

Implementer (IMP): turns concepts and plans into working procedures; plenty of self-discipline, combined with realistic, practical common sense; a practical organiser, translating policy decisions into easily understood procedures, then getting on with the work. This person likes structure and order and dislikes mess and chaos. Because of an essentially practical orientation, many nursery nurses are naturally in the Implementer role.

Monitor Evaluator (ME): this team member is particularly good at analysing problems and evaluating ideas and suggestions with an objective mind and the ability to think critically; able to analyse huge quantities of data; this person is most likely to identify the flaws in an argument and to stop the team from committing itself to a misguided project.

Team Worker (TW): this is often the most sensitive member of the group, very aware of the needs and worries of the other team members and is able to sense undercurrents; a good communicator; a good listener; he or she promotes unity and harmony so that the team, as a whole, works better when the Team Worker is there – things are different if he or she is absent.

Plant (PL): this team member contributes by putting forward new ideas and strategies; the most imaginative and intelligent member of the team, most likely to come up with radical new approaches; the person who is likely to provide the solution to a problem.

Belbin concluded that good teams would be much easier to form in organisations if thought were given to the team-role composition of natural working groups.